International Labour and Employment Compliance Handbook

Labour and Employment Compliance in Canada

International Bar Association

Labour and Employment Compliance in Canada

Second Edition

Kevin Coon
Adrian Ishak

This publication is part of the International Labour and Employment Compliance Handbook

Editors: Salvador del Rey and Robert J. Mignin

the global voice of the legal profession

Wolters Kluwer
Law & Business

Published by:
Kluwer Law International
PO Box 316
2400 AH Alphen aan den Rijn
The Netherlands
Website: www.kluwerlaw.com

Sold and distributed in North, Central and South America by:
Aspen Publishers, Inc.
7201 McKinney Circle
Frederick, MD 21704
United States of America
Email: customer.service@aspenpublishers.com

Sold and distributed in all other countries by:
Turpin Distribution Services Ltd.
Stratton Business Park
Pegasus Drive, Biggleswade
Bedfordshire SG18 8TQ
United Kingdom
Email: kluwerlaw@turpin-distribution.com

ISBN 978-90-411-5637-2

1. Argentina: Julio César Stefanoni Zani, Enrique Alfredo Betemps, *Labour and Employment Compliance in Argentina*, 2nd edition, 2014 (ISBN 978-90-411-5630-3)
2. Brazil: Sólon de Almeida Cunha, Jorge Gonzaga Matsumoto, Murilo Caldeira Germiniani, *Labour and Employment Compliance in Brazil*, 2014 (ISBN 978-90-411-4929-9)
3. Canada: Kevin Coon & Adrian Ishak, *Labour and Employment Compliance in Canada, 2nd edition*, 2014 (ISBN 978-90-411-5637-2)
4. Chile: Gerardo Otero A., Maria Dolores Dcheverria F., Macarena Lopez M. & Juan Pablo Cabezón O., *Labour and Employment Compliance in Chile, 2nd edition*, 2014 (ISBN 978-90-411-5633-4)
5. China: King & Wood Mallesons, *Labour and Employment Compliance in China, 2nd edition*, 2014 (ISBN 978-90-411-5631-0)
6. England: Tony Hyams-Parish, *Labour and Employment Compliance in England, 2nd edition*, 2014 (ISBN 978-90-411-5641-9)
7. France: Pascale Lagesse, *Labour and Employment Compliance in France, 2nd edition*, 2014 (ISBN 978-90-411-5639-6)
8. Germany: Gerlind Wisskirchen & Martin Lützeler, *Labour and Employment Compliance in Germany, 2nd edition*, 2014 (ISBN 978-90-411-5636-5)
9. India: Manishi Pathak, *Labour and Employment Compliance in India, 2nd edition*, 2014 (ISBN 978-90-411-5624-6)
10. Ireland: Duncan Inverarity & Sinead Grace, *Labour And Employment Compliance In Ireland*, 2014 (ISBN 978-90-411-5260-2)
11. Israel: Yaron Horovitz, Pnina Broder-Manor, Helen Raziel, *Labour and Employment Compliance in Israel*, 2013 (ISBN 978-90-411-4878-0)
12. Italy: Angelo Zambelli, *Labour and Employment Compliance in Italy, 2nd edition*, 2014 (ISBN 978-90-411-5632-7)
13. Japan: Yoshikazu Sugino, *Labour and Employment Compliance in Japan, 2nd edition*, 2014 (ISBN 978-90-411-5638-9)
14. Mexico: Oscar De La Vega Gómez & Monica Schiaffino, *Labour and Employment Compliance in Mexico, 2nd edition*, 2014 (ISBN 978-90-411-5643-3)
15. The Netherlands: Els de Wind, *Labour and Employment Compliance in the Netherlands*, 2013 (ISBN 978-90-411-4928-2)
16. Poland: Barbara Jóźwik, *Labour and Employment Compliance in Poland, 2nd edition*, 2014 (ISBN 978-90-411-5635-8)
17. Russia: Anna-Stefaniya Chepik, *Labour and Employment Compliance in Russia*, 2013 (ISBN 978-90-411-4925-1).
18. South Africa: Susan Stelzner, Stuart Harrison, Brian Patterson & Zahida Ebrahim, *Labour and Employment Compliance in South Africa, 2nd edition*, 2014 (ISBN 978-90-411-5640-2).
19. Spain: Salvador del Rey & Ana Campos, *Labour and Employment Compliance in Spain, 2nd edition,* 2014 (ISBN 978-90-411-5634-1)
20. United Arab Emirates: Sara Kohja, *Labour and Employment Compliance in the United Arab Emirates*, 2013 (ISBN 978-90-411-4966-4).
21. United States: Baker & McKenzie LLP, *Labour and Employment Compliance in the United States, 2nd edition*, 2014 (ISBN 978-90-411-5644-0)

International Bar Association
The Global Voice of the Legal Profession

The International Bar Association (IBA), established in 1947, is the world's leading organization of international legal practitioners, bar associations and law societies. The IBA influences the development of international law reform and shapes the future of the legal profession throughout the world. It has a membership of over 40,000 individual lawyers and almost 200 bar associations and law societies spanning all continents. It has considerable expertise in providing assistance to the global legal community.

Grouped into two divisions – the Legal Practice Division and the Public and Professional Interest Division – the IBA covers all practice areas and professional interests, providing members with access to leading experts and up-to-date information. Through the various committees of the divisions, the IBA enables an interchange of information and views among its members as to laws, practices and professional responsibilities relating to the practice of business law around the globe. Additionally, the IBA's high-quality publications and world-class conferences provide unrivalled professional development and network-building opportunities for international legal practitioners and professional associates.

The IBA's Bar Issues Commission provides an invaluable forum for IBA member organisations to discuss all matters relating to law at an international level.

The IBA's Human Rights Institute (IBAHRI) works across the Association, to promote, protect and enforce human rights under a just rule of law, and to preserve the independence of the judiciary and the legal profession worldwide.

Other institutions established by the IBA include the Southern Africa Litigation Centre and the International Legal Assistance Consortium.

Employment and Industrial Relations Law Committee

The aims of the committee are to develop and exchange knowledge of employment and industrial relations law and practice. Members support each other through the provision of innovative ideas and practical assistance on day-to-day issues. In addition, through its journal and through presentations, conferences, the committee ensures the dissemination of up-to-date law and practice in this highly important business area.

International Bar Association Global Employment Institute

The IBA Global Employment Institute (IBA GEI) was formed in early 2010 for the purpose of developing for multinationals and worldwide institutions a global and strategic approach to the key legal issues in the human resources and human capital fields.

Drawing on the resources and expertise of the IBA membership, the IBA GEI will provide a unique contribution in the field of employment, discrimination and immigration law, on a diverse range of global issues, to private and public organizations throughout the world. The IBA GEI is designed to enhance the management, performance and productivity of these organizations and help achieve best practice in their human capital and management functions from a strategic perspective.

The IBA GEI will become the leading voice and authority on global HR issues by virtue of having a number of the world's leading labour and employment practitioners in its ranks, and the support and resource of the world's largest association of international lawyers.

Further information

International Bar Association, 4th Floor, 10 St Bride Street, London EC4A 4AD, United Kingdom, Tel: +44 (0)20 7842 0090, Fax: +44 (0)20 7842 0091, E-mail: member@int-bar.org, www.ibanet.org

About the International Labour and Employment Compliance Handbook

From 1976 through 1988, the International Bar Association and Kluwer Law International published the groundbreaking International Handbook on Contracts of Employment. This Handbook provided one of the first global overviews of the law of the international employment relationship.

Since publishing the first edition, globalization of business has created an increased demand for knowledge of labor and employment laws throughout the world. Therefore, along with Kluwer, we decided to publish an updated Handbook which we have titled the International Labour and Employment Compliance Handbook.

This new Handbook was intended to be a practical guide by providing a general overview of key labor and employment issues in multiple jurisdictions. Each chapter was written so that it is easy to understand by lawyers and non-lawyers alike. Each country author has also followed a standard outline to assist readers in analysing employment issues in each country.

The first edition of this new Handbook included nineteen (19) different countries.

This Handbook would not have been possible without the help and assistance of many people. Most importantly, the individual country authors are all distinguished legal practitioners who spent considerable time drafting and revising their country reports to meet difficult deadlines. We thank each of them. Our friends at Kluwer, especially Ewa Szkatula, have done a wonderful job in keeping the editors and the authors on schedule. Finally, we want to also express our gratitude to Cuatrecasas, Gonçalves Pereira, and Baker & McKenzie LLP for their valuable assistance in the coordination and organization of this project. Our warmest thanks to each of them.

Because of the success of the Handbook,Wolters Kluwer Law & Business decided to publish each country report also as a separate book to give a choice in obtaining the information. We hope this new format will be a helpful and useful resource just like the Handbook. Both formats are available in print and online.

The Editors

Salvador del Rey Guanter
Robert J. Mignin

March 2013

Canada

AUTHORS

Kevin Coon CCEP

Kevin Coon is a member of the Labour, Employment and Employee Benefits Law Practice Group and is Managing Partner of the Toronto office of Baker & McKenzie LLP. Mr. Coon specializes in the interpretation and application of local and international labour and employment laws. He counsels, advises and trains executives, managers and supervisors in workplace due diligence, compliance, CSR, international and national labour standards, global labour relations, positive employee relations matters and best practices, as well provides representation and advocacy before various Courts, Coroners Inquests, Administrative Tribunals and Arbitrators.

Kevin received his law degree from the University of Western Ontario in 1987 and a Honours Bachelor of Arts Degree in International Relations and Economics in 1982. He has participated in Executive Leadership Training at the Kellogg Graduate School of Management in Chicago and at the Centre for Creative Leadership in Colorado.

Kevin has served terms working as a Policy Advisor to the Minister of Labour for the Government of Ontario, as an Assistant to the Minister of Justice and Attorney General of Canada and as a Special Constable with the Royal Canadian Mounted Police. He is actively involved with the United Nations International Labour Organization (ILO), as the Employer Representative on the Canadian Delegation including participation on the Committee on the Application of International Labour Standards, the Committee and drafting committee on the development of an international labour standard on HIV/AIDS and the World of Work and other initiatives. He also serves on the Working Group on Corporate Social Responsibility for the International Organization of Employers.

Kevin is certified as a Corporate Compliance and Ethics Professional (‘CCEP’) by the United States Society for Corporate Compliance and Ethics.

ADDRESS

Baker & McKenzie LLP
Brookfield Place
181 Bay Street, Suite 2100
P.O. Box 874
Toronto, Ontario M5J 2T3
Canada

Tel: +1-416-865-6941
Fax: +1-416-863-6275
E-mail: Kevin.Coon@bakermckenzie.com
Web: <www.bakermckenzie.com/>
CV: <www.bakermckenzie.com/kevincoon/>

Adrian Ishak

Adrian Ishak is a member of the Labour, Employment & Employment Benefits Group. Prior to joining Baker & McKenzie in 2008, he practiced with a large, full-service firm in Ottawa, Ontario.

Mr. Ishak provides strategic labour, employment and business advice to both domestic and international private and public sector employers. Mr. Ishak's practice encompasses all aspects of labour and employment law, with a particular emphasis on employment standards, labour relations and human rights in Canadian common law jurisdictions and Quebec's civil law jurisdiction.

ADDRESS

Baker & McKenzie LLP
Barristers & Solicitors
Brookfield Place
181 Bay Street, Suite 2100
Toronto, Ontario M5J 2T3
Canada

Tel: +1-416-865-6967
E-mail: Adrian.Ishak@bakermckenzie.com
Web: <www.bakermckenzie.com/>
CV: www.bakermckenzie.com/AdrianIshak/

Legal Compliance in Canada

Legal Compliance in Canada

1. LEGAL FRAMEWORK: EMPLOYMENT LAWS

Canada's employment law framework falls under a federal system. The majority of workers, upwards of 90%, are governed by provincial employment statutes. The other 10%, in defined industries considered to be of national interest (such as telecommunications, nuclear energy, shipping, or banking) are governed by federal employment statutes.

At either level, there are three sources for employment law. The first is statutory. Each jurisdiction has its own employment standards statute, as well as trade union, occupational health and safety, privacy, pension, and human rights legislation.

The second source is the common law. The judiciary of each jurisdiction applies common law principles (except the Province of Quebec which is based on a Civil Code), which are developed over time by judges, to employment cases brought before the courts. Unionized employees do not have access to the courts in the first instance because each jurisdiction in Canada has established mechanisms in its trade union legislation to direct disputes out of the court system and into private arbitration or the applicable administrative labour tribunal. The decisions of arbitrators and the labour tribunals are subject to a limited right of judicial review.

Finally, employment contracts, written or unwritten, are the third source of employment law in Canada. Judges interpret the terms of employment contracts, and arbitrators and labour tribunals interpret collective agreements for unionized workplaces.

All jurisdictions within Canada have set up various administrative tribunals to adjudicate claims that arise under various employment statutes, such as employment standards, workers' compensation, and human rights. These boards are meant to be less time-consuming and have less onerous requirements than courts to provide more open access for individuals.

Overall, Canadian employment law tends to be employee-friendly and imposes numerous obligations on employers to ensure the proper treatment of employees.

2. CONTRACTS OF EMPLOYMENT

2.1. Overview

Every Canadian employee's employment is governed by a contract, whether written or oral. There is no 'at-will' concept in Canadian employment law. The terms of an oral contract may be well known, with its terms expressly understood by the employee, or it may only be loosely understood or implied. Regardless of the form, there is always a contract and any attempt to unilaterally change or amend the contract could give rise to a breach of contract action or, where such change is material, a constructive dismissal action.

2.2. Written Employment Contracts

In Canada, the employment relationship is a contractual one. A written employment contract is not necessary, however, to create a relationship. A contract can be oral or written, and the terms of the agreement can be express or implied.

A written employment contract is advantageous in that it clearly sets forth the terms of the agreement between the parties. In a written contract, the employee and employer may agree to any provision that is not prohibited by law. Employment standards legislation sets out minimum contractual requirements which the parties cannot reduce. The employment contract can contain provisions in excess of the employment standards, and the parties may come to an agreement on issues that may be treated differently in the absence of an express agreement.

As courts often will impose a certain result in the absence of a specific agreement, there is an obvious benefit to ensuring that a contract clearly sets out the terms and conditions of employment. This is particularly the case with termination provisions that outline the amount of notice or pay in lieu of notice an employee would receive upon termination of employment, since, in the absence of contractual terms that indicate otherwise, the courts generally award significantly more than that required by applicable provincial employment standards legislation. Canada is not an 'at-will' jurisdiction for purposes of termination of employment.

Contracts generally contain provisions outlining remuneration for services rendered, the amount of notice (or pay in lieu of notice) that will be given in the event of termination of employment (unless the termination is for cause), and the employer's expectation of the faithful performance of the job's duties by the employee. If these terms are not expressly set out, they will be implied by the courts.

In most employment relationships, a simple contract that sets out the essential provisions will be sufficient to meet the needs of the parties. Where detailed employment agreements are unnecessary, an employment letter can be used to set out the key terms and provisions without the formality of a lengthy employment contract. For employment relationships that involve sophisticated compensation schemes, highly confidential business and trade secrets or unique features of the position, however, the parties would be wise to clearly articulate the parties' expectations in a contract that has been reviewed by the parties' respective legal advisors.

2.3. Oral Contracts

Oral contracts are sufficient to create a binding employment relationship. In the absence of express provisions, courts will use the common law to imply terms and conditions of employment.

Employers who have oral contracts with employees will have a difficult time requiring those employees to agree to written contracts later on in the employment relationship. It will be even more difficult if a long period of time has elapsed since commencement of employment. Employees are not obligated to sign a contract that changes any of the fundamental terms of their employment, and an employer's attempt to unilaterally introduce adverse terms of employment may give rise to an employee's action for breach of contract or constructive dismissal. Generally, employers will have to provide additional consideration for the new contract to be enforceable. Courts will not consider mere continuation of employment sufficient consideration.

2.4. Employee Handbooks

Employee handbooks are a commonly used tool in Canadian workplaces to set out the rules and policies that guide employees and management. Handbooks often contain extensive rules and policies specific to the operations of the employer. Handbooks are either expressly included in the employment contract or are implied as extended terms and conditions of the employment contract.

Reference to the handbook directly in an employment contract is beneficial as it sets out the rules and policies that must be adhered to and articulates the limits of acceptable behaviour for both parties. New employees should be given the handbook as soon as possible, and updates should be distributed to all employees promptly. Reference to the handbook in the employment contract can be used as evidence by the employer that the rules and policies of the employer are contractual conditions of employment. It is recommended, to the extent possible, that candidates for employment be given access, either in hardcopy or by electronic link to the employer's intranet, to the most up-to-date handbook and employer policies.

Employers are limited in how far they can amend, add or delete rules and policies from the handbook before it is considered a material change to terms and conditions of employment, which would require acceptance by the employee and possibly consideration. Employers who unilaterally introduce adverse terms and conditions to the handbook face the risk of a breach of contract or constructive dismissal claim by the employee. Alternatively, an adjudicator may determine that the change is not enforceable against the employee.

2.5. Job Descriptions

Job descriptions are an important indicator to applicants as to what the job entails and what the primary duties will be. As with other documents that form part of the employment relationship, a job description can be considered an implied component of the employment contract.

A legal issue that has arisen with respect to job descriptions is negligent misrepresentation on the part of the employer. Employers must be careful and ensure that the job description is an accurate indication of the work the applicant will be doing as an employee. It can be costly for the employer later on if the employer embellishes or misrepresents the duties and responsibilities of the position during the hiring process and the applicant relies on the representation to his or her detriment.

In a unionized setting, some collective agreements contain job descriptions, which outline the various tasks and responsibilities of unionized workers. Unions generally consider these job descriptions important as they are used by the union to protect union jobs by preventing managers from performing unionized employee work.

2.6. Offer Letters

Offer letters play an important role in the employment contract and should be drafted with the same care as a formal employment contract. An offer letter setting out the terms and conditions of employment will generally constitute the contract, unless a separate employment contract is subsequently signed by the parties and clearly states that it is the binding contract rather than the offer letter. If the employer drafts an offer letter and then has the employee sign a separate employment contract, the employer should ensure that there are no conflicting terms between the two documents. A more streamlined approach is to use one document that serves as both a more detailed offer letter and contains the required provisions of the employment contract.

Offer letters can be conditional, for example, on the results of a background check or the results of pre-employment testing. Once the conditions are met, in the absence of a subsequent contract contemplated by the parties at the time of the conditional offer letter, the offer letter will form part of the terms of the employment contract.

Courts expect the employer to be the more sophisticated bargainer and often will decide matters that turn on ambiguous or unclear language of the employment contract in favour of the employee. Employers can use language in the contract stating that the contract is the final and entire agreement and any prior agreements, written or oral, express or implied, are terminated upon the signing of the employment contract. To assist with the enforcement of such language, the employer should provide the final contract to the potential employee with sufficient time for the employee to review the contract and consult a legal advisor if he or she so desires. One to two weeks is not unusual and is favoured by the courts as a sufficient time period for an employee to review and consider whether to accept the offer.

Employment contracts that are signed *after* the employee commences work are typically unenforceable.

Other Documents

Other documents exchanged in the course of the employment relationship – particularly at the commencement of the employment relationship – may form part of the employment contract. Booklets or handouts that describe benefits programmes and pension plan documents are typical examples of documents that contain enforceable terms and conditions of employment. Unless such documents contain clear language that reserve to the employer the right to make changes in the future, the promises made in such documents are part of the employment contract.

2.7. Checklist of Do's and Don'ts

- Do consider a written employment agreement.
- Do review the job description prior to recruiting an employee.
- Do not make promises that cannot be kept.
- Do provide the employee handbook (and any policies that apply) at the time of hiring.
- Do provide updates to the handbook promptly.
- Do not forget that all documents provided to the employee during the hiring process can constitute part of the employment contract.

3. RECRUITING, INTERVIEWING, SCREENING AND HIRING EMPLOYEES

3.1. Overview

Employment recruiting in Canada is conducted directly by employers or by recruitment agencies acting on behalf of employers.

3.2. Recruiting

Employers use a variety of methods to recruit applicants. The internet has been a growing tool for years, and increasingly, social media plays a central role to both identify and to research candidates. Employers also use more traditional methods, such as newspaper and magazine advertisements, head-hunters, and employment agencies to fill gaps in their workforce.

Generally, the cost of recruitment cannot be passed down to applicants. That is, whether an employment agency is used or the employer recruits directly, applicants cannot be charged fees to apply for employment or when they are selected. The legislation is designed to prevent applicants from being exploited.

3.3. Employment Applications

Employment applications should focus on the information required to assess the qualifications and capacities of the applicant. Information used by an employer for the purposes of tax remittances or pension plan registration, such as date of birth and social insurance number (SIN), should only be requested after an offer has been made.

Applications for employment also should conform to human rights legislation and not solicit any information that would identify the applicant as a member of a protected group. Each province and the federal jurisdiction has legislation that sets out categories of groups protected from discrimination, which are similar, but do vary by jurisdiction and therefore must be consulted. Requesting such information that is not tied to the merits of the position exposes an employer to a claim of discrimination.

3.4. Pre-employment Inquiries

There are a number of pre-employment inquiries that employers are prohibited from making. Inquiries that would elicit information related to a prohibited ground of discrimination are not permitted. Such inquiries include those about age, race, gender, mental disability, physical disability, religion, sexual orientation, ethnicity, and national origin. Each province and the federal jurisdiction in Canada have enumerated prohibited grounds in their human rights legislation. Employers should ensure that their inquiries do not solicit information about any of the discrimination grounds. If an applicant volunteers such information, the best advice is to move the discussion to another topic and not to make a note of the volunteered information.

3.5. Pre-employment Tests and Examinations

Pre-employment tests used to measure the skills and abilities of applicants generally are permissible. The skills and abilities must be directly related to the position applied for.

The debate in Canada has focused on pre-employment drug and alcohol testing. Drug and alcohol testing for positions that are not safety sensitive has been controversial and subject to numerous legal challenges. In appropriate circumstances, such testing is permitted when the position for which the applicant is applying is a safety sensitive position, or if it is a bona fide occupational requirement. This is typically confined to positions that involve heavy machinery, the transportation of passengers or other positions that could put the employee, a co-worker or a member of the public at risk of physical injury. Requiring pre-employment drug and alcohol testing for a position such as a standard office job not involving any risk to the public will potentially attract liability under Canadian privacy laws.

The addiction to drugs or alcohol is considered a disability by human rights adjudicators in Canada. As a result, pre-employment tests for drug and alcohol for a position that is not a safety sensitive position may also expose an employer to liability under human rights laws.

3.6. Background, Reference, and Credit Checks

Background checks are a permissible form of employment screening in Canada, although some information may not be used to deny employment to a candidate. Criminal record checks are one form of background screening that can form the basis for a complaint to the human rights commission or tribunal within the jurisdiction. A few provinces include a conviction for which a pardon has been granted as a protected ground from discrimination. Several provinces prohibit using a criminal conviction as a reason to refuse to hire an applicant unless the employer can show that it is directly related to the position. The courts have made this test a difficult one for employers to meet. Provincial offences, which are not criminal in nature, also are protected grounds of discrimination in some provinces if they are not related to the requirements of the job. For example, multiple speeding tickets likely would be an impermissible consideration for the position of a receptionist, but for a long-haul trucker, it may be an important factor for employers to ensure public safety and minimize liability.

Background checks to ensure the information provided by an applicant is accurate is an often overlooked step in the recruitment process. The law in Canada is such that if an employee is discovered to have embellished or invented credentials in the recruitment process, but has performed satisfactorily in the position for a length of time, dismissal for cause may not be upheld by the courts. The dishonesty may not be enough to ground a case for dismissal depending on the time that has elapsed and the severity of the dishonest credentials.

Reference checks are permissible and generally considered an advisable practice for hiring managers. References are protected by qualified privilege, and an employer cannot be sued for defamation or libel from a past employee so long as it is the individual's honestly held opinion that is given. Despite this protection, some employers still are concerned about potential defamation claims and will limit the amount of information they provide to a prospective employer.

Some employers are also concerned that a future employer may sue them for misrepresenting the qualities and abilities of a past employee in a reference letter upon which the future employer relies. At this point, no court in Canada has permitted such a claim. There is some Canadian wrongful dismissal jurisprudence, however, that holds an employer liable for blocking an employee's attempt to secure new work if the employer unreasonably refuses to provide a reference when the employee was terminated from employment without cause.

The collection of background, reference and credit check information is governed by privacy and human rights laws that vary from province to province. Generally, applicants should be informed that the information will be collected and their agreement, in writing, should be procured prior to conducting any checks. Employers will need to check the appropriate jurisdiction's laws to determine if any privacy or human rights restrictions exist.

3.7. Interviewing

Employment interviews are a common method to screen applicants in Canada. With interviews, the main concern from a compliance viewpoint is that the questions do not infringe on an applicant's human rights. Every jurisdiction in Canada has a list of proscribed grounds of discrimination that vary, but generally include such categories as gender, age, race, religion, ethnicity, sexual orientation and disability. Interviewers cannot solicit information about any of the grounds of discrimination that are listed in the applicable human rights statute. The limited exceptions to this are where the particular ground is directly related to the requirements of the job. Employers may ask whether an applicant is of legal age to work in Canada or, for example, if the position is one serving alcohol, to ensure that the applicant is of the legal age to serve alcohol. On the other hand, asking an applicant what is his or her native language or where he or she went to high school may solicit information protected under the human rights laws and may expose the employer to a discrimination claim.

3.8. Hiring Procedures

Implementing standardized hiring procedures is a highly recommended practice for employers in Canada. By using a standardized procedure, employers can provide evidence to refute an allegation that there were improper considerations taken into account in the hiring process. Contracting out the recruitment process to an employment agency will not limit the liability of an employer, as the agency is considered to be an agent of the employer.

3.9. Fines and Penalties

Each jurisdiction has employment standards legislation that sets out the penalties that are payable if the employer does not meet one of its obligations under the legislation. Human rights legislation also provides for compensation to victims of discrimination.

3.10. Checklist of Do's and Don'ts

- Do determine prohibited grounds of discrimination within the jurisdiction.
- Do review application materials/interview scripts to delete inappropriate questions.
- Do ask for references.
- Do check references.
- Do get written consent to complete background checks.
- Do ensure that background checks are related to the merits of position.
- Do make offers conditional on satisfactory background check results.
- Don't engage in pre-employment drug or alcohol testing for non-safety-sensitive positions.
- Don't request information required for tax remittance/benefit plans until an offer of employment has been made.

4. MANAGING PERFORMANCE/CONDUCT

4.1. Overview

Performance management is a method to evaluate and monitor the general performance of an employee as well as to measure the specific performance around various company, workplace and career goals. It is an important part of the operation of any business.

Employers are afforded a great deal of latitude to manage their workplaces in the appropriate manner. Courts will not interfere with the business decisions of an employer, unless the employer does not live up to its legal obligations or interferes with the rights of employees. Courts often rely on performance management documentation when adjudicating disputes regarding termination of employment for cause. Courts now demand that employers engage in some form of performance management prior to terminating employment for poor performance. Similarly, human rights adjudicators will look to performance management documentation as one indicator that any adverse job action was not founded on discriminatory grounds.

4.2. Coaching and Counselling

Coaching and counselling are important steps in performance management. Providing feedback to employees allows them to identify areas of strength and weakness. Coaching is an opportunity to develop employees' skills, but it also lays the groundwork for justifying dismissal if an employee's performance does not improve.

Employers should ensure that coaching sessions are documented. Documentation provides a written record of expectations, goals, achievements and requirements. In order to respond to an allegation of wrongful dismissal, documentation of coaching is crucial. Given the requirement to warn under-performing employees that their employment is at stake prior to termination of employment, records of coaching can confirm a pattern of poor performance and provide evidence that the employee received warnings that their employment is in jeopardy.

4.3. Written Evaluations

Performance appraisals are another useful tool in managing performance. Reviews at regular intervals help track improvement and achievements, allow the employer to document areas of poor performance, and provide warning of the employee's unsatisfactory work. Performance appraisals, however, are only useful tools if they are undertaken honestly and fairly. Too often managers will rate most, if not all, employees as satisfactory either because of a lack of time to undertake a true evaluation or the human tendency to avoid conflict with others. Courts are not receptive to an argument that years' worth of satisfactory performance appraisals should not be relied upon because the employer did not put the time or effort into honestly evaluating the employee.

4.4. Warnings and Suspensions

Where incompetence or on-going performance issues are the basis for the decision to dismiss an employee, courts have held that the employee is entitled to a fair warning of the potential termination of employment prior to effectuating a dismissal. Employees are entitled to be told that their job is in jeopardy if there is no improvement and given a reasonable amount of time to improve. Where the employee has breached his or her duty of honesty or fidelity (i.e., theft or fraud), a warning may not be necessary as the employee has effectively repudiated the contract.

Progressive discipline is the practice of engaging in progressively more serious exercises of discipline to manage employee behaviour. Originally, progressive discipline was followed only in unionized environments, however, it has become more common in non-union workplaces. Progressive discipline policies can help an employer demonstrate just cause in a wrongful dismissal action. A policy on discipline that is distributed to employees and consistently implemented by the employer is a recommended practice.

One aspect of progressive discipline, a suspension without pay, is a subject of debate in the non-union environment. Currently, the common law does not permit suspensions without pay in non-union workplaces. Suspensions must be expressly or impliedly included as a term and condition of employment to be upheld in court. Suspensions can be implied through evidence of either the intention of the parties or the applicable custom and usage. They also can be implied by law where it is considered necessary for the proper functioning of the employment contract.

4.5. Checklist of Do's and Don'ts

- Do include coaching to manage performance.
- Do take performance appraisals seriously and accurately evaluate employee performance.
- Do make a performance management policy.
- Do distribute the performance management policy to employees and provide it to new employees.
- Do implement the performance management policy consistently and uniformly.
- Do ensure that every warning or act of discipline is documented.
- Do determine if unpaid suspensions are incorporated into the employment contract.
- Do provide a reasonable amount of time for an under-performing employee to improve.
- Do warn employees that termination is possible if there is not sufficient improvement.

5. TERMINATION OF EMPLOYMENT OF EMPLOYEES FOR PERFORMANCE OR DISCIPLINARY REASONS

5.1. Overview

Employees who are terminated from employment for performance or disciplinary reasons are said to be terminated for 'cause' or in the union environment with 'just cause'. Most termination litigation turns on the question of whether the employer had cause to terminate the employee's employment. If cause is found, then the employer has no obligation to the employee beyond paying wages and any other amounts earned and owed up to the date of termination of employment. If there is no cause for dismissal, the employer has an obligation to provide reasonable notice of termination or pay in lieu of notice. In the non-union environment, wrongful dismissal cases are litigated in the courts. It is considered difficult to prove cause, especially for performance reasons, as the courts have set a high standard for proving such claims. The defendant employer has the burden in court to prove that there was cause for termination.

5.2. Separation Pay

When an employee is terminated with cause, the employer is not obligated to provide any notice of termination, pay in lieu of notice nor reasonable notice of termination.

Where the termination is without cause, the employer has both a statutory obligation to provide notice and/or pay in lieu of notice and a common law obligation to provide reasonable notice of termination. Each jurisdiction in Canada has a statutory provision that requires a minimum amount of notice of termination that is based on the employee's length of employment. Two weeks notice for employees with more than one year of service, but less than three, is a typical amount. The amount increases with length of service. Ontario has an additional statutory requirement for an employer with a two-and-one-half million dollar annual payroll in Ontario to provide 'severance pay' equal to one week per year of service, pro-rated for partial years, to a maximum of twenty-six weeks, for employees with five or more years or service.

The common law entitlement to reasonable notice usually goes further than the statutory entitlement. Typically, the common law notice for termination will be in the range of two to six weeks for each year of service, inclusive of the statutory entitlements, based on the factors outlined below. The maximum ceiling is around twenty-four months notice (although some awards have gone higher).

The Supreme Court of Canada has outlined four factors to consider in determining the length of reasonable notice. The first factor is the age of the departing employee. The second is the years of service of employee. The greater the length of employment or age of the worker, the more notice is required. The third factor is the character of employment. If it is a senior position, or one where the skills are highly specialized and narrowly applicable to other areas of work, this suggests an increased notice period. A low-level position, or one with widely transferable skill sets, indicates a shorter notice period. The final factor is the availability of similar employment. More notice is required where there are not many options for re-employment.

Employees, however, have an obligation to mitigate their damages to the best of their ability. If the employee does not attempt to seek other employment, or makes a poor attempt, then the court can decrease the amount of notice for failure to mitigate. The policy rationale for the obligation to mitigate is to provide an incentive for employees to replace their lost income and prevent the need to go to court to claim damages.

5.3. Fines and Penalties

There are fines and penalties when provisions of the employment standards legislation are not followed. Such statutory fines and penalties are not available at common law, although punitive damages are available to punish employers who engage in particularly harsh and reprehensible conduct. While recent jurisprudence has made it more difficult for employees to successfully claim damages for such harsh and reprehensible behaviour, the risk remains for employers who engage in such conduct.

5.4. Checklist of Do's and Don'ts

- Do document reasons for termination of employment.
- Do conduct an investigation into alleged misconduct prior to terminating.
- Do interview witnesses to any misconduct.
- Don't assume the employer can terminate anyone at any time for any reason.
- Do determine the severance/termination pay obligations in employment standards legislation.
- Do consider the potential common law reasonable notice liability.
- Don't withhold owed wages or accrued vacation pay from an employee terminated from employment for any reason.

6. LAYOFFS, REDUCTIONS IN FORCE, AND/OR REDUNDANCIES AS A RESULT OF JOB ELIMINATIONS OR OTHER RESTRUCTURING

6.1. Overview

Layoffs, reductions in force and redundancies result when employment of one or more employees is suspended or terminated for business reasons, such as eliminating unnecessary positions, slowing down of business or interruption in work. Reductions in force refer to the permanent downsizing of a workforce. Layoffs may be temporary for an indefinite amount of time or they may evolve into permanent termination. Such terminations often results from attempts to make businesses more economically competitive by reducing costs.

6.2. Reductions in Force/Layoffs/Job Eliminations

A reduction in force refers to a permanent reduction in the total number of employees. Reductions in force may include seasonal, temporary or on call employees. The federal government has initiated a 'Work Force Reduction' programme. Employers who enter into the programme provide benefits to employees who agree to leave their jobs as a result of a reduction in force. Workers who agree to leave their jobs may receive Employment Insurance (EI) benefits as long as they are eligible.

EI is a federal programme that provides income to workers who are unemployed while they search for new employment. Although EI is a federally-governed programme, it applies to both federally and provincially governed workers and workplaces. Eligible workers are entitled to EI benefits if the workers lose their job through no fault of their own (i.e., due to a shortage of work or seasonal or mass lay-off), and they are available for and able to work but cannot find jobs. If the worker voluntarily quits his or her job or is fired because of misconduct, the worker is not entitled to EI benefits.

To be eligible for EI, the employee must show that he or she has been without work and without pay for at least seven consecutive days and has worked for the required number of insurable hours in the last fifty-two weeks since his or her last claim. This period is called the qualifying period. The minimum insurable hours are based on where the claimant lives and the unemployment rate in the claimant's economic region at the time of filing.

The term layoff traditionally refers to a temporary interruption of work. Recently, however, the term also has referred to permanent elimination of employment. A temporary layoff is when a job is not ended permanently, but is suspended, cut back or temporarily stopped. Generally, when there is a temporary layoff the employee is not entitled to receive any notice, any reason for the temporary layoff, or any indication of a date as to when the employee will be called back to work. It should be noted, however, that in the absence of language in the employment contract or collective agreement, it is a breach of the implied contract to layoff an employee without pay. Layoffs should be avoided if the employer is simply looking to delay a certain termination of employment.

In the event the employment contract or collective agreement does permit layoffs, temporary and permanent layoffs are regulated by employment standards legislation in each province. In the unionized context, employers may have bargained with the union regarding the terms that will be followed when a layoff is contemplated. Often, seniority of the employees is a determining factor in who will be laid off first.

A permanent reduction in force may be regulated more closely by the government, particularly if a large number of employees are affected. The employer may be obligated to provide relevant information to the government prior to the reduction. Employers considering a layoff should consult the applicable employment standards legislation to determine their obligations to employees and note any notice provisions which require communication with the government. The *Canada Labour Code*, for example, provides that a federally-regulated employer who terminates fifty or more employees within a four week period must give written notice to the Minister, the trade union (if the employees are unionized), and the affected employees at least sixteen weeks in advance of the termination date. In non-unionized workplaces, the written notice must be communicated to affected employees by posting it in conspicuous places.

Temporary layoffs do not require the employer to pay severance or termination pay or to provide reasonable notice *in lieu* of pay. Under the Ontario *Employment Standards Act*, a temporary layoff is considered one of the following:

(a) a lay-off of not more than thirteen weeks in any period of twenty consecutive weeks;
(b) a lay-off of more than thirteen weeks in any period of twenty consecutive weeks, if the lay-off is less than thirty-five weeks in any period of fifty-two consecutive weeks and: (i) the employee continues to receive substantial payments from the employer; (ii) the employer continues to make payments for the benefit of the employee under a legitimate retirement or pension plan or a legitimate group or employee insurance plan; (iii) the employee receives supplementary unemployment benefits; (iv) the employee is employed elsewhere during the lay-off and would be entitled to

receive supplementary unemployment benefits if that were not so; (v) the employer recalls the employee within the time approved by the Director; or (vi) in the case of an employee who is not represented by a trade union, the employer recalls the employee within the time set out in an agreement between the employer and the employee; and

(c) in the case of an employee represented by a trade union, a lay-off longer than a lay-off described in (b) above, where the employer recalls the employee within the time set out in an agreement between the employer and the trade union.

An employer is deemed to have terminated the employee if the employee is laid off for a period longer than the period of a temporary layoff. Once a temporary layoff becomes permanent, the employer's obligations to dismissed employees are triggered, including notice or pay in lieu of notice.

6.3. Fines and Penalties

Employment standards legislation may hold the employer liable for failure to adhere to the legislation. For example, in Ontario, if an employment standards officer finds that a person has contravened the *Employment Standards Act*, the officer may order the person to cease contravening the provision, order action for the person to take or refrain from taking to comply with the provision, and specify a date by which the employer must take action. In British Columbia's *Employment Standards Act*, a person whom the director determines has contravened any provision of the *Act* is subject to a monetary penalty prescribed by the regulations.

6.4. Checklist of Do's and Don'ts

- Do provide the applicable government body with relevant information if the employee reduction is permanent and involves the minimum number of employees contemplated by the applicable employment standards legislation.
- Do ensure that proper notice is made to the government authorities if the layoff requires notice.
- Do determine whether a layoff is temporary.
- Do provide at least the minimum statutory severance pay, termination pay or reasonable notice in lieu of pay if an employee has been terminated from employment.
- Don't contravene applicable employment standards acts nor the common law regarding layoffs and workforce reductions.

7. LABOUR AND EMPLOYMENT LAW RAMIFICATIONS UPON ACQUISITION OR SALE OF A BUSINESS

7.1. Overview

Acquiring or selling a business may be a wise decision if the employer wishes to enter into a new market or expand its workforce. However, both the company selling and the company acquiring the business must consider myriad issues when it comes to the legal entitlements of affected employees.

An employee's legal entitlements will differ depending on whether the business transaction is a sale of shares or an asset purchase. If the corporate change is a sale of shares, the transaction is merely a change in shareholders and there will be no change in the corporate identity of the employer. In this case, no termination of employment is triggered by the corporate transaction and any individual employment agreements and/or collective bargaining agreements in force will continue in effect after the sale of shares. The employees continue to be employed under the same terms and conditions after the sale of shares. Should the corporation want to terminate any employees during or after the sale of shares, the usual notice or pay in lieu of notice is required.

On the other hand, if the corporate change is a sale of some or all of the assets of the business, the corporate identity of the employer is generally deemed to have changed, and employees will be entitled to notice of termination of employment or pay in lieu of notice. The policy reasons behind this distinction is that a person's contract of employment is not transferable from one legal entity to another without the consent of the employee.

Practically speaking, in the context of an asset purchase, if the employee(s) consent to transferring to the new employer, then notice of termination of employment or pay in lieu of notice will not be required.

If the workplace is unionized, whether the corporate transaction is a sale of shares or an asset purchase, labour legislation deems the company to whom the business has been sold to be bound by the collective agreement as if the company had been a party to the agreement initially. In other words, the purchasing company effectively steps into the shoes of the target company when it comes to labour relations. In labour relations terms, the new business is a 'successor employer'.

7.2. Acquisition of a Business

Whether the corporate transaction involves a sale of shares or an asset purchase, planning the merger or acquisition of a business involves several human resources and employment law issues. The purchaser should engage in careful and detailed due diligence to ascertain whether the target company has a union, as well as, what are the terms of any individual employment contracts, benefit agreements or pension plans that may flow with the deal to the purchaser.

If purchasing some or all of the assets of the corporation, detailed negotiations will need to occur regarding the employment status of the affected employees. If the purchaser wants to retain the employees, it will have to formally offer new employment, and any employee who declines the offer will be entitled to notice or pay in lieu of notice of termination of his or her employment with the seller. Unless negotiated for otherwise, the seller will be liable for providing the notice or pay in lieu of notice, as the employment contract cannot automatically transfer to the purchaser without an employee's consent.

Purchasers need to ensure that the government registrations that existed prior to the asset purchase are changed to reflect the new corporate identity/employer for employees retained through a new offer of employment. This can include the payroll registration for Canada Pension Plan, EI, and other federal government remittances; workers' compensation registrations; employer health tax registrations; and any other mandatory or optional registrations.

7.3. Sale of a Business Checklist

A company should consider the following steps when selling or purchasing business, whether the corporate transaction is a sale of shares or a sale of assets:

- Remember that statements made to employees pre-acquisition may result in legally enforceable obligations.
- Confirm whether any terms and conditions of employment (other than the employer's name) will change as part of the integration of the old business with the new business.
- Confirm if there will be an actual vacation time/pay reduction as compared to any other benefit enhancements. For each employee, determine the actual financial impact of the changes to compensation. If further terms and conditions of employment will change, it will be necessary to determine exactly which terms and conditions are affected and consider whether such changes would be considered 'material' at law. If such changes are 'material', further steps may be necessary because the changes could trigger constructive dismissal claims if not handled properly. Additionally, in an asset purchase, any 'material'

changes must be communicated to the employees being offered a position in the new corporate entity so that the parties are not exposed to either misrepresentation or constructive dismissal claims.

- Collect and review collective agreements and individual employment agreements and terms and conditions of employment to determine whether there are any provisions which would trigger payments and/or other entitlements and/or prevent the purchasing company from offering employment on new terms.
- Review benefit and pension plans and arrangements (if any) of employees of the company being sold to determine whether such plans have provisions that would trigger payments and/or other entitlements and/or prevent the purchasing company from offering employment on new terms.
- Determine the compensation and benefit plans of the employees to whom employment will be offered (if different from what is already in place), or, in the case of a share transaction, of any employees affected by the corporate transaction.
- Analyse and compare compensation and benefits on an employee-by-employee basis.
- Decide what consideration, if any, will be offered for the new employment contracts.
- Confirm employees of the company being sold will be able to automatically participate in the purchasing company's benefit plans, if necessary, including whether providers need any particular information or individual employee consent.
- Confirm with payroll provider/insurance provider/tax and workplace insurance authorities which notifications are required.
- Determine whether any employees of the company being sold are on a work visa or permit. Contact government agencies and arrange for transfer of any work visas or permits.
- Determine whether there are any fixed term agreements, independent contractor agreements or outsourcing agreements. Review such agreements to determine potential liability. Decide whether to continue (novate or assign) or terminate these agreements, in accordance with the terms.
- Prepare and deliver offer of employment or notice of termination of the fixed-term, independent contractor and outsourcing agreements, or prepare and execute novation agreements for agreements with fixed term, independent contractors and outsourcing companies.
- In the case of an asset purchase, contact relevant provincial workplace safety and insurance boards to arrange for the closing of the sold company's accounts and the account transfer of any employees moving to the new corporate entity.

8. USE OF ALTERNATIVE WORKFORCES: INDEPENDENT CONTRACTORS, FIXED-TERM CONTRACT EMPLOYEES, AND TEMPORARY OR LEASED WORKERS

8.1. Overview

Aside from employees employed on a contract of indefinite duration, there are other categories of workforce personnel that a company may utilize to meet its labour needs. Independent contractors, fixed-term contract employees and temporary or leased workers are used to supplement or replace work conducted by a company's employees. The decision to use one type of alternative workforce may depend on several factors, including the duration and size of the project, the company's budget, the need for expertise in a particular field, and the nature of the company's business.

8.2. Independent Contractors

a. Definition

An independent contractor is a person, business or corporation that provides goods or services to another entity under terms specified in a contract or within a verbal agreement. Unlike an employee, an independent contractor does not work regularly for an employer, but works as and when required.

b. Creating the Relationship

Although Canadian jurisprudence has stated several tests for determining the existence of an independent contractor-client relationship, the central question is whether the person engaged to perform services is performing them as a person in business on his or her own account. Courts tend to consider four factors when determining whether an entity is an independent contractor or an employee. While not an exhaustive list, the test commonly examines:

(i) the degree or absence of control exercised by the alleged employer;
(ii) ownership of the tools necessary to do the work;
(iii) who bears the chance of profit and risk of financial loss; and
(iv) the degree to which the individual's work is integrated into the alleged employer's business.

If the terms of employment are self-directed, then the entity likely is an independent contractor. Independent contractors usually have their own tools of the trade and bear a greater risk of financial loss. Typically, if the work is not integral to the functioning of the business, the entity conducting the work will be an independent contractor. The total relationship between the parties must be considered to determine whether an entity is an independent contractor.

c. Compensation

Compensation should be specifically addressed in the service contract. The contract should specify the fees to be paid and when such fees will become payable during the term of the contract. Remuneration may be on an hourly, fixed fee/lump sum, cost plus basis, or percentage of the project cost. Remuneration typically is higher for independent contractors than for employees for the same job because the independent contractor must cover his or her own overhead costs. The independent contractor should not receive bonuses or benefits. He or she is paid only for work completed. Income taxes and worker's compensation insurance are deemed the personal responsibility of the independent contractor and are not deducted at source.

d. Other Terms and Conditions

The following terms and conditions typically are found in a contract for an independent contractor: the specific term and duration of the contract, the specific services the independent contractor will provide, the fees charged by the independent contractor, an explicit statement of the nature of the relationship between the parties, a confidentiality agreement, an assignment of intellectual property rights, grounds of termination of the contract; and general contract provisions.

8.3. Fixed-Term Contract Workers

A fixed-term contract employee is not an independent contractor, but an employee. The term 'contract employee' typically refers to an employee with an employment contract for a fixed term. For example, some employees have employment contracts for one year, which may or may not be renewed at the end of the year. These employees are entitled to all minimum employment standards except notice of termination, unless employment terminates prior to the end of the employment contract. Under the common law, if a fixed-term contract employee is terminated without cause prior to the end of the employment contract, the employee may be able to sue for lost income for the remainder of the contract. Where the employee has a fixed-term contract and it is renewed more than two to three times, courts will likely look beyond the contract and find the relationship actually was one of indefinite duration where the employee is entitled to reasonable notice of termination where the termination is not for cause.

8.4. Temporary or Leased Workers

A temporary or leased worker is an individual who provides services for a business, but who is an employee of and is paid by, a separate specialty agency or leasing company. The agency or leasing company is responsible for administrative matters, including statutory payroll withholdings such as income tax, Canada Pension Plan and EI remittances; vacation pay, as well as any optional employment benefits such as pension, medical, dental or disability insurance. Temporary or leased workers are considered employees of the leasing company for tax and benefit purposes. However, should the temporary or leased worker work within an organization and become an integrated member of the organization for an extended period of time, the risk arises that the temporary or leased worker may eventually be deemed an employee of the organization.

8.5. Checklist of Do's and Don'ts

- Do consider whether the use of alternative workforces is necessary given the specific project.
- Do stipulate the term of employment/service, fees and compensation, intellectual property rights, and liability of the independent contractor, fixed-term contract employee or temporary/leased employee.
- Do consider the duration of time that the employer will require the services of an independent contractor, fixed-term contractee or temporary/leased employee.
- Do not let the person work longer than the term stipulated in the contract, unless the term of the contract has been formally renewed.

9. OBLIGATION TO BARGAIN COLLECTIVELY WITH TRADE UNIONS: EMPLOYEES' RIGHT TO STRIKE AND A COMPANY'S RIGHT TO CONTINUE BUSINESS OPERATIONS

9.1. Overview of Employees' Right to Organize

Every Canadian worker possesses a constitutional right to organize. This includes a right to join a union, to organize meetings and activities having to do with labour issues and to select union leaders to represent employees' interests. Employees also have a right to use union power to make requests related to their employment. Furthermore, employees have the legislative right to organize action to compel an employer to change or improve its terms and conditions of employment.

There are a number of steps unions take to organize a workplace. These usually include building a union organizing committee, identifying workplace issues, obtaining signatures on union cards, launching a union campaign and negotiating a contract after a successful campaign.

9.2. Right of Employees to Join Unions

In every Canadian jurisdiction, an employee's right to join a union ('freedom of association') and the right to free collective bargaining is set out in statute. In Ontario these rights are found in the provincial *Labour Relations Act*, which states that every person is free to join a trade union of the person's own choice and to participate in its lawful activities. The Ontario Labour Relations Board (OLRB) is an agency of the Ontario government. It oversees most of the collective bargaining that takes place in Ontario. Similar legislation and administrative labour relation bodies exist throughout Canada at the provincial and federal level. The jurisdiction of such boards are determined by the nature of the work performed by the employees in the proposed bargaining unit, namely whether the workplace is provincially or federally regulated.

Employers are prohibited from interfering with unions. This means that employers cannot interfere with union meetings or activities or restrict employees' union rights. Typically, it is illegal for an employer to do any of the following to an employee seeking to join a union:

- refuse to employ or dismiss an employee because of union participation;
- discriminate against an employee based on union membership;
- attempt to restrain an employee from joining a union;

– penalize an employee who seeks union membership;
– intimidate or coerce an employee to prevent the employee from joining a union;
– refuse to acknowledge a certified trade union.

9.3. How Employees Select Unions

A union may be local, provincial, national, international, or an independent organization that represents the employees of a type of business or trade. There are very few independent unions remaining. Economies of scale have made it more common for unions to amalgamate or for smaller unions to be absorbed into larger national unions.

Any group of workers can establish their own union. This is done by drafting a constitution and bylaws, enrolling members, electing officers and filing the appropriate documents with the applicable labour relations board.

Today, most employees who seek union membership will join an established union. This process generally is considered to be easier and more efficient and, most importantly, it provides employees and workers with the support of a pre-existing organization familiar with labour processes. Employees generally choose unions based on their interests and the degree to which the union's goals and principles align with those interests. Many unions are industry-specific to ensure that they understand the needs and specific interests of their members. However, unions may attempt to organize workers outside of their known industries, especially as many of the traditionally strong unions suffer membership decline due to significant workforce reductions within their industries.

9.4. Campaigning

In order to win union rights for a group of employees, called a bargaining unit, a union will launch a campaign. In a campaign, a union will request that members of the prospective bargaining unit sign union membership application cards. The union then will present the cards to the applicable labour relations board. The board decides if a vote should be held in order to determine if the majority of the employees want union representation. The time period between a union's application for certification of a bargaining unit and the vote to determine if a certificate will be issued is referred to as the campaign period.

Each Canadian jurisdiction has its own rules for union certification. In Ontario, the union must ensure that at least 40% of the employees in the prospective bargaining unit have signed union cards. After this number is reached, a vote can be held. However, in other jurisdictions, a unionization vote is not required if a certain percentage of employees have signed union membership cards. For example, under the federal *Canada Labour Code*, a union can be automatically certified after more than 50% of employees sign membership cards. Once the threshold has been met, the federal labour board will issue a certificate. If the union does not have enough signatures for automatic certification, it still may have enough signed cards to compel a vote.

Both unions and employers may use certain tactics and strategies during the campaign period. While unions are likely to launch organizing strategies, employers may launch resistance or anti-union campaigns. There are rules surrounding what an employer may do during the campaign period. For example, employers cannot conduct surveillance, make promises, or intimidate or threaten employees in an effort to influence employee decisions. If an employer uses any of these tactics and a complaint is filed, the labour relations board which adjudicates the dispute may take action. Punishment for such action may include automatic certification, also known as penalty or remedial certification, of the union. The policy rationale for automatic certification is that where an employer has so poisoned a work environment, the workers will no longer be able to express their true wishes through an anonymous vote because of the fear and concerns instilled by the employer.

Following certification, the employer and union must bargain in good faith in an effort to reach a collective agreement. Failure to bargain in good faith is considered an unfair labour practice.

9.5. Unfair Labour Practices

An unfair labour practice is a violation of any provision of provincial or federal labour relations legislation and may be committed by an employer, employers' organization, trade union or individual. Generally, scrutiny for unfair labour practices has focused on the employers, with less concern for union unfair labour practices.

Complaint mechanisms are in place through the provincial and federal labour boards to have alleged cases of unfair labour practices reviewed. If the labour board rules that the conduct constitutes an unfair labour practice, it will intervene and order an end to that practice.

Some examples of unfair labour practice include:

- interfering in the organization or administration of a union;
- interfering with a union's ability to represent its members;
- preventing an employee from joining a union;

- preventing an employee from participating in union activities;
- threatening, discriminating against, or intimidating an employee because of actual or perceived union activity;
- negatively adjusting an employee's schedule because of actual or perceived union activity;
- terminating an employee because of actual or perceived union activity.

9.6. Relocation of Work/Shutdown of Business

The relocation of work or the shutdown of a business may be subject to provincial or federal labour relations legislation. The law on this issue recently was tested in Quebec. The Supreme Court of Canada confirmed that a court cannot question the reasons behind a company's decision to shutdown or relocate work. However, a shutdown must be genuine. Management cannot temporarily close a business simply to avoid dealing with a union. Closure will not constitute an unfair labour practice if the employer knows that it cannot meet the union's demands and closes the store as a better alternative to a prolonged strike without the reasonable prospect of securing a settlement which would allow it to remain economically viable. However, the onus is on the employer to demonstrate that the closure of the business was for legitimate business reasons. Where the evidence clearly indicates that the sole purpose of the employer's closure is to rid itself of the union and its supporters, an unfair labour practice is found. Such actions on the part of the employer would not meet the test of genuineness.

9.7. Checklist of Do's and Don'ts

It is important for the employer to understand its duties when it comes to union organizing. Labour relations legislation encourages open communication between the employer and the union. Employers may wish to discuss general issues surrounding union organization with their employees. However, employers should avoid holding closed-door or captive audience meetings with employees as these could be interpreted as acts of coercion. At the very least, closed-door meetings may suggest that the employer is exerting undue influence on employees. In all communications, it is imperative that the employer avoid coercing, intimidating or unduly influencing employees.

- Do present your case for a non-unionized workplace in an objective, neutral manner.
- Do allow employees to discuss wages and benefits.

- Do negotiate collective agreements in good faith once a union bid is successful.
- Don't interfere with employees' activities with unions.
- Don't interfere with employees marking campaign ballots during a campaign.
- Don't discuss union bids with employees in a closed office.
- Don't actively discourage employees from supporting the union.

10. WORKING CONDITIONS: HOURS OF WORK AND PAYMENT OF WAGES

10.1. Overview of Wage and Hours Laws

The federal and provincial governments govern wage and hour requirements through employment standards legislation. Ceilings are placed on the maximum number of hours an employee may work in a day or week. Minimum wage requirements establish a floor and ensure that an employee always will be entitled to a certain minimum amount of remuneration for his or her services. These wage and hour standards ensure a fair and equitable work environment and are meant to correct any power imbalance existing between the employer and the employee.

10.2. Minimum Wage

The provincial jurisdictions all have minimum wage legislation. The federal jurisdiction applies the minimum wage of the province in which a worker is employed. In 2014, minimum wage ranges from USD 9.50 (CAD 9.95) to USD 10.72 (CAD 11.00) and fluctuates from time to time. Parties are prohibited from contracting out of the minimum wage requirements stipulated for that jurisdiction. However, parties are able to negotiate more favourable contractual arrangements. It is important to note that if an employer contracts with an employee to provide a higher wage than the minimum, the employer will be held to that wage rate.

Generally, it is an offence for an employer to allow an employee to work for less than minimum wage. Tips and gratuities are excluded from the calculation of minimum wage. Employers must pay employees, in industries where tipping is common, the minimum wage without taking into account the amount received in tips. It is common, however, for the minimum wage rate in such industries to be set at a slightly lower rate by the legislation to account for the likelihood of tips and gratuities.

10.3. Overtime

The right to overtime pay is tied to hours of work provisions. On average, most jurisdictions hold that if an employee works more than eight hours per day or forty hours per week, the rate of overtime pay is one and one half times the regular rate of pay. Typically, an employee cannot be compelled to work more than eight hours per day or forty-eight hours per week. The employer and employee can enter into an agreement to vary this 'ceiling' if necessary. Each province has set its own requirements for overtime and maximum hours of work, so each jurisdiction's legislation must be consulted prior to permitting overtime work.

10.4. Meal and Rest Periods

In most Canadian provinces, there is some regulation on how long an employee may be compelled to work without being granted a meal or break period. Employees usually are entitled to at least one thirty minute rest break for every five hours of work. Most provinces allow employers to apply to a designated administrative authority for a permit varying the rest break requirements. Generally, employers cannot force an employee to remain on company property during meal breaks; however, there are exceptions to this rule and the applicable provincial legislation should be consulted.

10.5. Deductions from Wages

Most provinces have legislation expressly prohibiting deductions from wages unless such deduction is specifically permitted by statute or by a specific written agreement of the employee. For example, the federal *Canada Labour Code* permits deductions to be made for any reason provided that the employee gives a written authorization permitting the deduction. Such authorization must not have occurred through duress or intimidation.

Notwithstanding the statutory prohibition against wage deductions, the employer is entitled to bring a civil suit to recover damages for items such as mistaken overpayments, faulty workmanship, and misappropriation of company property.

10.6. Garnishment

Garnishment of wages occurs when the employee owes another party money but has not satisfied the debt. The creditor may intercept the money that would have been paid to the employee and have it paid into court. Garnishment always is done by court order. Once an employer is served with a garnishment order, the employer must comply with the order, regardless of any contradictory instructions made by the employee. Garnished wages are always paid into court. It is not paid directly to the creditor. The debt must be owing at the time the garnishment order is delivered to the employee.

The employment standards legislation in the federal jurisdiction as well as the majority of the provinces makes it unlawful for an employer to dismiss, suspend, discipline, lay off or otherwise penalize an employee on the ground that garnishment proceedings are likely to be commenced or have commenced. As garnishment orders are made to enforce the repayment of a debt, there is a policy rationale to ensure that the ability to pay is maintained. Accordingly, reprisal has been prohibited through legislation.

10.7. Exemptions to Wage and Hour Laws

Typically, legislation expressly excludes specified benefits from the definition of wages. For example, ‘wages’ may exclude tips and other gratuities, expenses and travelling allowances, employer payments to a benefits plan, or benefits under such a plan which an employee is entitled to receive.

Certain industries and occupations are excluded from the maximum hours of work and overtime pay provisions. Some of the exemptions may include depending on the province: taxi drivers; defined qualified professionals such as lawyers, doctors, accountants, optometrists, surveyors and engineers; fisherman and hunters; defined construction workers; teachers in schools, colleges and universities; police, firefighters and security personnel and railway workers. Salespeople, who earn their wage through commission, often are exempted from certain provisions in employment standards legislation.

10.8. Child Labour

An employment contract cannot be enforced against a minor child unless either: (1) the contract is for ‘necessaries,’ as that term is understood in law; or (2) the contract as a whole is for the benefit of the infant; or (3) the infant ratifies the contract, expressly or constructively after attaining the age of majority.

If the court regards the contract as not being in the infant's overall best interest, it will be declared void. If the entire contract is voided, the infant cannot keep those terms in the contract which are favourable while rejecting those that are not. The question of whether the contract is beneficial must be considered at the time the contract was made. If the arrangement would have appeared beneficial to reasonable people at the time it was made, it does not matter that a subsequent turn of events has made it less beneficial to the infant.

An infant may recover for unpaid wages. However, since the infant lacks legal capacity, the infant may have to bring any court action through his or her parent or guardian. Some provinces have enacted special legislation which permit minors to sue for wages as if they were of age of majority.

10.9. Recordkeeping Requirements

a. Information That Must Be Maintained

Employers are required to maintain certain information on each employee from the moment of hiring. The *Canada Pension Plan Act* requires that all employers obtain an employee's Social Insurance Number (SIN) immediately upon hiring. The *Employment Insurance Act* requires that employers retain information such as books of account detailing remuneration paid to employees and the employee's SIN until either six years have elapsed from the end of the year to which the records relate or until permission is obtained from the Minister allowing the employer to dispose of the records. Electronic records must be kept for the same time period. Details on the specific information that must be retained by the employer are listed below.

b. Records That Must Be Retained

Record-keeping duties imposed on the employer are similar for each province. The *Canada Labour Code* is indicative of the typical record-keeping duties that provincial employment standards statutes impose on employers. These obligations include maintaining records of employee's wages, hours of work, general holidays, annual vacations and conditions of work for at least thirty-six months after the relevant work has been performed. Regulations pursuant to the *Canada Labour Code* provide further record-keeping requirements. Additional record maintenance requirements include SINs, occupational classification, sex and age, rate of wages, wage computation formulas, daily hours, actual daily earnings, details of every deduction, written agreements between the employer and the employee, dates for vacations and maternity/paternity leaves, pay periods, notices of termination, and explanations for employee absences.

c. Failure to Maintain Required Records

A representative of the Minister of Labour and the Canada Revenue Agency may enter the employer's premises and examine the employer's books and records at any time. The employer is obligated to produce any information required by the representative. Failure to assist in the inspection or to furnish information is an offence punishable by law.

The provinces also require that records be available for inspection. The applicable employment standards legislation prescribes penalties for failure to maintain the records as required.

10.10. Reductions in Compensation Caused by Economic Downturn

There may be several options available to employers who wish to reduce compensation during an economic downturn. One option is to reduce or forfeit overtime pay. Provided there are no contractual provisions to the contrary, an employee has no right to work overtime. The employer could hire additional employees to perform work at a regular rate.

Other options that involve some risk of a constructive dismissal claim include changing the structure of bonuses and base salary and placing greater emphasis on performance based remuneration. The employer could also reduce or eliminate items such as travel allowances, club memberships and bonuses. An employer also may consider 'across the board' reductions or freezes in salary.

Typically such reductions should affect all employees and should not be reduced by more than 5% to 10% of the employee's salary. Sufficient notice of the reduction or freeze should be given to the employee to diminish the likelihood of constructive dismissal claims. A constructive dismissal claim would arise when the employee alleges that the reduction in pay was a material change to a fundamental term or condition to employment without consent. Therefore, the employee could consider the employment contract repudiated, thus entitling the employee to the same damages as if he or she had been wrongfully dismissed.

10.11. Checklist of Do's and Don'ts

- Do abide by statutory minimum wage and maximum hour laws.
- Do allow workers to have the requisite meal and rest periods.
- Do deduct from wages only in accordance with statutes.
- Don't make non-statutory deductions without the employee's written consent or agreement through the employment contract.
- Don't threaten an employee with suspension, termination or other form of penalty if it appears that garnishment is imminent or has commenced.
- Do abide by child labour laws.
- Do maintain appropriate records for the appropriate time period.
- Do carefully assess alternatives to reduction in compensation in times of economic downturn.

11. OTHER WORKING CONDITIONS, BENEFITS AND LEAVES OF ABSENCES

11.1. Health and Other Insurance

A common company policy is the provision of employee health benefits through an independent insurance agency. Although Canadians are covered by a universal health care system, there are still many health related items that are not covered by the universal health care system but that may be covered through a private plan. For example, private health insurance may provide nearly complete reimbursement for the following costs: accidental dental coverage covering damage to natural teeth; partial reimbursement for ambulatory services; braces and splints; diabetic supplies; dental care; drugs; hearing aids; massage therapy; medical equipment such as wheelchairs; treatment by a licensed speech therapist, licensed clinical psychologist, registered chiropractor, osteopath, chiropodist or podiatrist; physiotherapy; private duty nurses; prosthetic appliances; and vision care. Private health insurance coverage could also include an accidental death or dismemberment benefit to be paid to the policy holder or the policy holder's spouse and dependent child. Employers may pay all, part or none of the premiums for the employee.

Long-term disability and short-term disability benefits may also be provided for under private health insurance policies. Long-term disability is when the employee is limited from performing the material and substantial duties of his or her regular occupation due to sickness or injury for an extended period of time. The definition of long-term disability will vary according to the insurers' policy. Insurance companies may calculate monthly disability payments by multiplying earnings at or below a threshold amount by a certain percentage, then multiplying earnings above a certain threshold by another percentage, and finally adding those two amounts together. Monthly earnings are considered monthly income, before deductions for federal and provincial taxes. It generally does not include income received from commissions, bonuses, overtime pay, or any other extra compensation or income received from sources other than the employer. The maximum monthly benefit payment typically is capped at a certain amount depending on the terms of coverage. The employee must be under the regular care of a physician in order to provide confirmation of disability.

Short-term disability provides the employee with a partial replacement of lost income if the employee is temporarily unable to work due to becoming totally disabled. It covers injuries and illnesses not related to work, and bridges the period until the employee is able to return to work or until long-term disability benefits start. This period is typically two to three months long. While long-term disability is almost always provided for by a third party insurance company, some companies will self-fund their own short term disability plan.

Life insurance coverage provides financial assistance to an employee's family members after the employee's death. The life insurance contract will set out how much money family members will receive, how much the employer will pay each month in order to provide insurance coverage (i.e., premium), and how long the insurance will cover the employee.

11.2. Pension and Retirement Benefits

All employees, with the exception of those in Quebec which has its own pension system, have the benefit of drawing from the *Canada Pension Plan*. The *Canada Pension Plan* entitles employees, upon retirement or disability, and the widows, widowers, and orphans of deceased employees, to a pension. The *Canada Pension Plan* pays 25% of an employee's average pensionable earnings, up to a maximum of approximately USD 950 per month. The employer is required to make sure that every employee 18 years of age or older has applied for a Social Insurance Number (SIN). A SIN is required if an individual wishes to work in Canada and to have access to government programmes and benefits. The employer also is obligated to deduct money from the employee's wages in order to contribute to the *Canada Pension Plan*. The money deducted from an employee's wages is held in trust for the employee and forms no part of the employer's accounts. Employees also can take advantage of private pension funds which are employer-sponsored, such as a group Registered Retirement Savings Plan

(RRSP), or their own private RRSP or other retirement savings plan to supplement the pension that they will receive from the federal government.

11.3. Vacation and Holiday

Generally, the employer is obligated to pay the employee his or her vacation pay before the vacation period commences. The period in which the employee must be paid prior to vacation ranges from one working day to two weeks. Each jurisdiction has created its own provisions to calculate vacation pay. The amounts that are and are not included in vacation pay are set out in employment standards legislation. Calculating vacation pay may include overtime earnings, bonuses, commissions, and holiday pay. In Ontario, vacation pay is equal to at least 4% of the wages, excluding vacation pay, which the employee earned during the period for which the vacation is given.

Both federal and provincial legislation stipulates that certain days of the year are public holidays. If the employee is required to work, employers must pay their employees at a specified premium rate. Generally, the premium is the payment of a regular wage plus 1.5 times thereof. If the employee does not work on the holiday, he or she is entitled to regular pay for that day. In most jurisdictions, the employee must have been working for the employer for a specific amount of time before he or she is entitled to take statutory holidays. This time period ranges from thirty days to three months. In most provinces, the employee must have worked on the last day before and first day after the statutory holiday in order to qualify.

Public holidays typically include: New Year's Day, Good Friday, Victoria Day, Canada Day Labour Day, Thanksgiving Day, Family Day and an August civic holiday also are included in some provinces. The federal jurisdiction also has its own public holidays.

Employment standards legislation requires that employees are paid accrued vacation and holiday pay upon termination of employment. The period of time for which pay is owed is calculated by examining the employee's pay record to determine what amount of vacation or holiday pay he or she has received in preceding years and for which qualifying periods of time. In Ontario, if an employee is terminated, the employer pays any wages to which the employee is entitled not later than the later of seven days after the employment ends and the day that would have been the employee's next pay day. Any accrued vacation or holiday pay amounts must be paid to the employee despite any amounts outstanding that the employee may owe the employer.

11.4. Leaves of Absence

Many types of absences are covered by employment standards legislation. Legislation has expanded the types of absences that are protected. This protection is beneficial to employees. The statutes include provisions that prohibit reprisal solely because the employee exercised his or her right to take a leave protected by the legislation. This has allowed employees to attend to important life events without fear that their employer may terminate their employment for being away from the workplace. For most leaves, an employer is required to provide unpaid time off without penalty. For certain leaves, such as maternity and paternity leave, the employee may be eligible to apply for benefits under the federal employment insurance scheme.

a. Personal Leave

Employment standards legislation does not specifically entitle an employee to take personal leaves of absence. These types of leaves are granted at the discretion of the employer. The employee may require personal leave due to emergency and non-emergency unforeseen circumstances, personal or family responsibilities, or educational obligations. If the leave is requested due to a ground protected under applicable human rights legislation, such as religious observances, the employer may have to accommodate to the point of undue hardship. Requests for personal leave need not be granted with pay.

b. Medical or Sick Leave

Most Canadian jurisdictions have employment legislation entitling employees to receive unpaid sick leave. The employee must have accrued a minimum amount of work hours ranging from thirty days to six months before becoming entitled to sick leave days. Where there is legislation governing sick leave, an employer is prohibited from terminating, suspending or dismissing an employee because he or she has been absent due to illness for less than the maximum period specified in the statute. Sick leave is typically without pay, although if the illness requires a longer time off, the employee may be able to access the company's short-term disability benefits, if applicable. In other jurisdictions which do not have legislation for sick leave, the employee may have grounds for a wrongful dismissal suit if the employer dismisses the employee due to sick leave, particularly if the absence is due to a disability rather than a temporary illness. Contractual terms may entitle an employee to specific amounts of sick leave. Often such contractual terms are implied under the common law.

When an employee's absence is due to disability, the employer will have an obligation under human rights legislation to accommodate the employee's disability to the point of undue hardship.

If the employee's medical condition results in a permanent disabling illness, the employer may have grounds for termination of the employment contract due to frustration. Employers should proceed with extreme care if considering such an action, as human rights obligations in this area create a high threshold for employers before termination of employment is permissible.

Courts have ruled that the test for frustration of the employment contract is as follows: Was the employee's incapacity looked at before the purported dismissal, of such a nature, or did it appear likely to continue for such a period, that further performance of his obligations in the future would either be impossible or would be radically different from that undertaken by him and accepted by the employer under the agreed terms of his employment? The court then articulated five factors which increase the likelihood of frustration: first, the presence of a relatively short notice of termination period; second, the fact that entitlement to sick pay has expired; third, a short expected duration of the employment in the absence of sickness; fourth, the fact that the employee occupies a key post in which he must be replaced on a permanent basis; and fifth, the fact that the period of past employment is relatively short.

c. Bereavement Leave

The majority of provincial governments and the federal government provide an employee with time off in the event of the death of defined relatives. Traditionally, the term 'defined relatives' is restricted to mean the employee's natural family and/or his or her family through marriage or adoption. Recently, 'defined relatives' has been expanded to mean multi-generational families and common-law and same-sex relationships. Bereavement leave generally is unpaid. It is typically reserved for workers who have been employed in their current job for three consecutive months. The duration of leave periods ranges from one day to one week.

d. Family Leave

Many jurisdictions provide employees with a maximum period of unpaid compassionate leave in emergency situations. The situation must involve a defined family member who is facing significant risk of death within twenty-six weeks of either the date of a certificate provided by a doctor or the commencement of leave. The maximum leave period is eight weeks. The employee must provide the employer with advance notice of his or her intention to take leave. The employee does not receive wages during the leave, but he or she is entitled to receive benefits under the federal *Employment Insurance Act*. These benefits may be collected for a maximum period of six weeks. Some provinces allow for leave in a broader range of circumstances, such as health or education reasons.

e. Pregnancy Leave

All provinces and the federal jurisdiction have legislation entitling women to a leave of absence for childbirth and protecting women against penalties with respect to their job tenure and other terms, conditions and benefits of employment because of pregnancy.

The majority of provinces provide for seventeen weeks of unpaid leave. This time period may be extended if a doctor certifies that an employee's medical condition renders her unfit to return to work. In all jurisdictions, an employee can extend her pregnancy leave by taking a parental leave (see below), which is thirty-seven weeks in most jurisdictions. If the employee uses parental leave this way, the parental leave will begin immediately upon the expiration of pregnancy leave. The employee's combined maximum leave period is usually fifty-two weeks.

The employer is not required by legislation to provide pregnancy leave with pay. Instead, the federal employment insurance schemes (provincial if in Quebec) provide financial assistance to the employee.

Most jurisdictions require a minimum period of prior employment with the employer to qualify for pregnancy leave.

f. Parental Leave

Employees entitled to take parental leave include a birth parent, an adoptive parent, or a person who is in a relationship of some permanence with a parent of the child and who plans on treating the child as his or her own. This includes same-sex couples.

The length of parental leave varies with each jurisdiction, with the average time being thirty-seven weeks. The employer is not required to pay for parental leave. However, the employee can apply for benefits under the federal employment insurance legislation (provincial, if in Quebec).

An employee may take a leave of absence upon the adoption of a child under all provincial and federal jurisdictions. Generally, there are no distinctions between adoption leave and parental leave.

g. Injury at Work

If an employee is injured at work, and needs to leave work to seek medical attention, the employee is entitled to the rest of the day's wages. The policy rationale for this is to ensure that employees seek medical attention. In the absence of fear of losing a day's wages, it is believed that employees will be more likely to seek treatment.

For more on work-related injuries and illnesses, please see section 12 below, 'Workers' Compensation'.

h. Military Leave

Protection of an employee who is absent due to military duties is protected by provincial employment standards acts. Under the Ontario *Employment Standards Act*, an employee is entitled to a leave of absence without pay if the employee is a reservist and will not be performing the duties of his or her position because the employee is deployed to a Canadian Forces operation outside Canada, or the employee is deployed to a Canadian Forces operation inside Canada that is or will be providing assistance in dealing with an emergency or its aftermath. Upon the conclusion of an employee's leave due to military obligations, the employer shall reinstate the employee to the position the employee most recently held with the employer, if it still exists, or to a comparable position, if it does not. Further, the employer shall pay a reinstated employee at a rate that is equal to the greater of the rate that the employee most recently earned with the employer or the rate the employee would be earning had he or she worked throughout the leave. Failure to afford the employee with these rights violates employment standards legislation.

11.5. Checklist of Do's and Don'ts

- Do deduct from an employee's wages in order to contribute to the *Canada Pension Plan* and *Employment Insurance*.
- Do provide an employee who is terminated from employment with holiday and vacation pay.

- Do provide employees with those leaves protected by statute in the applicable jurisdiction.
- Do abide by workers' compensation schemes in the event that an employee is injured in the course of employment.

12. WORKERS' COMPENSATION

12.1. OVERVIEW

All provinces have enacted workers' compensation schemes to compensate employees who have been temporarily or permanently disabled by accidents or diseases in the course of their employment. Workers' compensation legislation provides a comprehensive and exclusive scheme to adjudicate workplace accidents.

Employers who participate are protected from any liability that arises as a result of workplace accidents and illnesses. Co-workers, other employers and other workers also are exempt from liability. Where an employee has the opportunity to pursue a claim civilly, such as an automobile accident in the course of employment, the provincial legislation requires the worker to elect to claim benefits or to pursue the claim in a civil proceeding. The provinces all have entered into inter-jurisdictional agreements with one another so if a worker covered in one province is injured in the course of employment in another province, the worker will be able to claim for benefits.

The requirement to participate and pay premiums into the workplace insurance system varies by province. In some provinces almost all employers must participate with very few industries exempted. In others, numerous industries are exempted from participating. Workers' compensation allows voluntary registration for employers in exempted industries who wish to have protection from liability.

Workers' compensation legislation provides six main categories of benefits: income-replacement benefits, permanent impairment benefits, death benefits, medical aid, rehabilitation services, and the right to return to work post-injury. Income-replacement benefits allow the employee to be paid a percentage of lost earnings. The percentage varies in each province. Permanent impairment benefits are awarded based on the employee's continuing pain and suffering. The payment usually is paid periodically, but workers can request commutation of benefits to a lump sum. Death benefits, or survivor benefits, are given to the surviving dependents of the deceased. These benefits are paid immediately upon death. Medical aid pays the health-care and related costs associated with workplace injuries. Rehabilitation services provide assistance to a worker who is unable to return to pre-injury employment because of a permanent injury.

Rehabilitation provides training in other areas of employment so the worker may return to employment in some capacity, either with the pre-injury employer or with a new employer. The right to return to the pre-injury employment is a relatively new benefit that currently is available in certain provinces. The right to return protects the worker from the loss of his or her job as a result of an injury or illness until the worker is prepared to return to the pre-injury position.

12.2. Checklist of Do's and Don'ts

- Do determine if the industry is exempted from coverage.
- Do consider optional coverage for exempted industries.
- Do determine if the employee was in fact injured during the course of employment.
- Don't ignore accident reporting requirements.
- Do ensure that all injury reporting forms are properly completed.
- Do participate with return to work programmes.

13. COMPANY'S OBLIGATION TO PROVIDE SAFE AND HEALTHY WORKPLACE

13.1. Overview of Safety and Environmental Laws and Regulations

Every province has an occupational health and safety act. The legislation governs the obligations placed on employers and employees for the maintenance of a safe and healthy work environment. In addition, there are several regulations under the acts. In Ontario, for example, there are regulations for industrial establishments; construction projects; mines and mining plants; health care and residential facilities; workplace hazardous materials; critical injuries; biological and chemical agents; designated substances such as arsenic, asbestos, benzene, lead, and mercury; diving operations; protective equipment for firefighters; offshore oil and gas; window cleaning and confined spaces. Federal safety guidelines are found under the *Canada Labour Code*.

13.2. Requirements

All injury prevention statutes combine an external and internal system. The external system establishes minimum standards for workplace health and safety, while the internal system prompts employers and employees to assume certain responsibilities for promoting health and safety.

The external system is governed by the applicable occupational health and safety legislation. The legislation stipulates that employers comply with the following requirements. First, employers must ensure that the health and safety of every employee at work is protected. Second, the employer must comply with a list of specific duties. These duties include implementing a health and safety policy and programme; ensuring that building structures, equipment, ventilation, heating, sound, lighting, humidity and temperature meet prescribed standards; providing employees with the prescribed safety clothing and equipment; providing prescribed safety training and relevant health and safety information; reporting accidents in the prescribed manner; ensuring the safety of all entrances and exits; making sure that all employees are aware of every known or foreseeable health safety; ensuring that the activities of persons granted access to the workplace do not endanger the health and safety of employees; complying with strict labelling and warning rules for hazardous materials; disclosing information relating to the contents of prescribed controlled products to a physician for the purpose of treating employees in emergency situations; and finally, allowing an employee to refuse to perform work that the employee reasonably believes is too dangerous.

Recent amendments to the *Criminal Code*, expanded a company's liability upon failing to provide a safe workplace. Section 217.1 of the Code states: 'Every one who undertakes, or has the authority, to direct how another person does work or performs a task is under a legal duty to take reasonable steps to prevent bodily harm to that person, or any other person, arising from that work or task.' The new section 217.1 indicates that an organization can be found guilty of criminal negligence where the physical act and the mental intent are perpetrated by two separate people in the organization. It is not necessary that the 'directing mind' of the company possessed the mental intent in addition to commissioning the physical act. This erodes the insulation which traditionally protected companies from liability. As a result, both individuals and organizations can be convicted of criminal negligence for failure to abide by the duty outlined in section 217.d.

For individuals, the maximum penalty for criminal negligence causing death is life imprisonment, and the maximum penalty for criminal negligence causing bodily harm is ten years' imprisonment. However, individuals are subject to a range of *Criminal Code* sentencing options, including absolute discharge, probation, and prison. The sentence depends on the circumstances of the crime. Organizations, including corporations, are subject to a maximum fine of USD 100,000 where the Crown proceeds by summary conviction (the least serious manner of proceeding). Where the

Crown proceeds by indictment, which would occur in more serious circumstances, there is no limit on the amount of the fine for the corporation.

In the internal system, workers assume responsibility for the health and safety standards unique to their organization. Provincial legislation contains statutory minimums which cannot be eliminated through contract. For example, the *Occupational Health and Safety Act* in Ontario requires that joint health and safety committees meet at least once every three months. The federal *Canada Labour Code* also imposes certain duties on joint committees for federal undertakings. These include the duty to receive and address complaints relating to health and safety; maintain records pertaining to such complaints; cooperate with any occupational health service provided at the work place; participate in all inquiries and investigations; regularly monitor programmes, measures and procedures; ensure the adequacy of records; and cooperate with safety officers. The decisions of joint committees are recommendations and are not binding on management. The parties, however, are free to expand the statutory minimum obligations.

13.3. Rights of Employees

The employee possesses two principal rights: the right to refuse dangerous work and the right to know workplace hazards.

The worker has the right to refuse to do work that he or she genuinely believes to be dangerous. The employer does not have the right to dismiss an employee who refuses to do work based on this ground. The federal *Canada Labour Code* exemplifies the Canadian system and enunciates two steps for the employee to follow when refusing what he or she perceives to be dangerous work. First, the worker must have reasonable cause to believe that the work constitutes a danger to the employee or to other employees. The employee may not refuse work if the refusal would put the life, health or safety of another person directly in danger or if the danger in question is a normal condition of employment. In Ontario, the standard for determining the reasonableness of the employee's refusal is subjective. The worker must have an honest and genuine belief that the work asked of him or her was unsafe. There are slight variations among the provincial statutes as to the employee's subjective belief. Second, once a worker possesses the reasonable cause to refuse work, he or she must report the refusal to the employer. If the employer finds that the work was, in fact safe, the standard then becomes objective. According to the OLRB, the objective standard is whether the average employee at the workplace considering his or her general training and experience and, exercising his or her normal and honest judgment, would have reason to believe that the circumstances presented an unacceptable degree of hazard to himself or herself or another employee.

The employee also possesses the right to know workplace hazards. For example, under the *Canada Labour Code*, one of the employer's specific duties is to ensure that each employee is made aware of every known or foreseeable health or safety hazard in the area where the employee works.

13.4. Duties of Employer

The burden of ensuring a safe workplace falls on the employer. Employers are responsible for the acts of managers, agents, representatives, officers and directors. The employer has the right to be shielded from liability provided that its duties are fulfilled.

The employer has the duty to provide a safe workplace. For example, under the Ontario *Occupational Health and Safety Act*, the employer must ensure that: (i) the equipment, materials and protective devices as prescribed are provided; (ii) the equipment, materials and protective devices provided by the employer are maintained in good condition; (iii) the measures and procedures prescribed are carried out in the workplace; (iv) the equipment, materials and protective devices provided by the employer are used as prescribed; and (v) a floor, roof, wall, pillar, support or other part of a workplace is capable of supporting all loads to which it may be subjected without causing the materials therein to be stressed beyond the allowable unit stresses established under the *Building Code Act*.

The employer must comply with regulations made pursuant to the provincial occupational health and safety acts. Regulations may cover topics such as the control of designated substances or particular activities carried out at the workplace.

The employer must provide information to and educate workers. This duty to educate includes acquainting workers with any workplace hazards and acquainting persons such as supervisors or managers with potential hazards.

The employer must appoint a competent supervisor. Under the *Ontario Occupational Health and Safety Act*, a competent person means a person who: (i) is qualified because of knowledge, training and experience to organize the work and its performance; (ii) is familiar with this Act and the regulations that apply to the work; and (iii) has knowledge of any potential or actual danger to health or safety in the workplace.

Furthermore, the employer is bound to comply with certain obligations. In Ontario, for example, some of these obligations include the following:

– The employer shall create a written occupational health and safety policy and develop a programme to implement that policy. The policy should cover who is affected by the policy, who will be held accountable for breaches of the policy and penalties for a breach of the policy. The employer must provide training for workers, supervisors and committee members in order to carry out the policy's mandate and post a copy of the provincial health and safety act in the workplace in both French and English.

- The employer has the duty to take every reasonable precaution to ensure the health and safety of its workers. This duty is extended to include management of sexual harassment, fear of workplace violence and harassment, protection of workers in isolation, and tobacco exposure.
- If the workplace uses biological, chemical and physical agents, the employer will incur a variety of duties, including: overseeing the handling, storing, use and disposal of such agents; keeping records of which employees are exposed to the agent; notifying a Director of the use or introduction of such agent; monitoring the levels of agents used in the workplace; and complying with a standard limiting the exposure of a worker to such agents.
- Employees must be provided with written instructions regarding company safety measures and procedures.

In the event an employer is reprimanded for a violation of a duty to provide a safe workplace, the employer possesses the right to raise a defence of due diligence. The employer must prove that reasonable steps were taken to protect the employee before the incident occurred. Courts have considered the following factors when assessing the viability of an employer's due diligence defence: the knowledge of workplace hazards, the gravity of the potential harm, the employer and employee's compliance with external workplace standards created by government regulation, the existence of a system for reducing workplace hazards, and the presence of a functioning occupational health and safety system.

13.5. Specific Standards

Provincial regulations fix minimum standards for a variety of operational and procedural matters. Regulations address the operation of work processes, permissible chemicals and materials, manufacturing and operating standards for equipment and machinery, the maintenance of on-site medical and sanitary facilities, maintenance of periodical medical check-ups, hazard identification, warning employees of hazards, and warning employees about the minimum qualifications required for a particular employment.

The Workplace Hazardous Materials Information System (WHMIS) is Canada's national hazard communication standard. WHMIS is implemented through federal, provincial and territorial legislation. Supplier labelling requirements are set out under the *Hazardous Products Act* (HPA) and associated Controlled Products Regulations administered by Health Canada. The key elements of the system are cautionary labelling of containers of WHMIS 'controlled products', the provision of material safety data sheets and worker education and training programmes.

Suppliers and employers must ensure that containers of a hazardous substance other than controlled products are labelled to disclose the name of the substance and the hazardous properties of the substance.

The employer must obtain a copy of the material safety data sheet providing background information on the substance and make the data sheet readily available in the workplace for examination by employees.

Controlled products under the legislation require a supplier material safety data sheet or a workplace material safety data sheet, either of which should be readily available for examination by employees, the safety and health committee or health and safety representatives.

13.6. Injury or Accident at Work

Under provincial occupational health and safety legislation, an inspector or officer may investigate an injury or accident occurring in the workplace. For example, the *Occupational Health and Safety Act* of Alberta states that if an accident occurs at a work site, a government appointed director or occupational health and safety officer may attend at the scene of the accident and make any inquiries the officer considers necessary to determine the cause of and circumstances surrounding the accident. The officer may request information from any individual who was at the scene of the accident or has knowledge of the accident. An officer may seize or take samples of any substance, material, product, tool, appliance or equipment that was present at, involved in, or related to the accident. The officer will provide a receipt for any samples taken during the investigation to those from whom samples were taken and will return such items when the investigation has concluded. The officer may enlist the help of a peace officer in conducting the accident investigation. Similar powers are bestowed upon safety officers in other provinces.

For more information, please see above, section '12. Workers' Compensation.'

13.7. Workplace Violence and Harassment

Workplace violence encompasses several types of conduct. It may include violence between co-workers, violence between an employee and a customer, or violence between an employer and an employee. It generally includes violence leading to actual physical injury, as well as attempts and threats of physical injury. The obligation to provide a violence-free workplace has been subsumed under the employer's general duty to use every precaution available to provide a safe work environment for the employee. However, provincial jurisdictions, as well as the federal government, have proposed legislation which would create a specific statutory duty to protect workers from workplace violence. In Ontario, Bill 168, which went into effect in June 2010, made significant changes to the law. The Bill requires employers to commit to the development and implementation of a policy and prevention programme with respect to workplace violence and harassment. The violence and harassment prevention programme must include procedures for reporting violence and harassment, investigating and remedying such complaints, and training workers to ensure their familiarity with the policy and programme.

13.8. Fines and Penalties

The provincial acts make it an offence to violate legislative provisions. For example, in Ontario, every person who fails to comply with a provision of Act or the regulations, an order or requirement of an inspector or a Director, or an order of the Minister is guilty of an offence and, on conviction, is liable to a fine of not more than CAD 25,000 or to imprisonment for a term of not more than twelve months, or to both. If a corporation is convicted of an offence, the maximum fine that may be imposed upon the corporation is CAD 500,000.

13.9. Checklists of Do's and Don'ts

- Do abide by federal and provincial statutes and regulations pertaining to occupational health and safety.
- Do investigate claims of unsafe work.
- Don't engage in reprisals against employees who refuse unsafe work.
- Do provide a healthy and safe work environment for employees.
- Do implement a policy addressing health and safety issues, and in certain jurisdictions ensure that workplace violence and harassment are specifically addressed.

- Do educate employees as to both their and the employer's rights and obligations for promoting a safe work environment.

14. IMMIGRATION, SECONDMENT AND FOREIGN ASSIGNMENT

14.1. Overview of Laws Controlling Immigration

The Canadian *Immigration and Refugee Protection Act* ('IRPA') provides that no person other than a Canadian citizen, a permanent resident or those in possession of a work permit may lawfully engage in employment in Canada. Certain types of work are exempted from the need for a work permit, ranging from business visitors and after sales service, to clergy and diplomatic work. These exceptions are listed in section 186 of IRPA.

14.2. Recruiting, Screening and Hiring Process

The government sets strict requirements for recruitment advertising for employers seeking to hire temporary foreign workers, and these requirements change regularly. The requirements should be reviewed before undertaking any recruitment effort that may result in hiring foreign workers. If an employer receives an application from a suitable foreign employee, the employer and foreign worker are then subject to the rules of the federal 'Temporary Foreign Worker Program'. This program allows eligible foreign workers to work in Canada for an authorized period of time, if employers can demonstrate that they are unable to find suitable Canadians or permanent residents to fill the jobs. Employers also must prove that the entry of these workers will not negatively impact the Canadian labour market. Foreign workers can be recruited for most types of businesses.

There are four steps to hiring a temporary worker through the standard process

First, the employer must determine if it requires a Labour Market Opinion ('LMO') from the government to temporarily employ the worker. Categories of workers which usually require an employment confirmation include live-in caregivers, seasonal agricultural workers and workers in highly-skilled or management-level occupations.

Second, the employer must apply for the LMO, if required. Service Canada will consider the following factors when administering a LMO: the occupation in which the foreign worker will be employed; wages and working conditions offered to the foreign worker; the employer's advertisement and recruitment efforts to hire Canadians or permanent residents; associated labour market benefits that may occur from hiring the foreign worker; and determination if the entry of the foreign worker will likely affect the settlement of an ongoing labour dispute.

Third, the employer notifies the foreign worker that he or she must complete the work permit application, which is then processed by Canada Border Services Agency if the individual is visa-exempt, with an additional requirement to go to a Citizenship and Immigration Canada visa office if the individual requires a visa. The foreign worker must include proof of identity, a valid passport or travel documents, a copy of the job offer or signed employment contract, and a copy of the positive LMO, or documentation proving how he/she qualifies under an LMO exemption.

Some types of work permit are LMO-exempt, including those issue under international free trade agreements, intra-company transferees and post-graduation work permits for foreign students.

Permanent Residency

A foreign worker may apply to be a permanent Canadian resident. Skilled workers are selected as permanent residents based on their education, work experience, knowledge of English and/or French, and other criteria that have been shown to help them become economically established in Canada. A foreign worker's application for permanent residency may be processed if he or she has an offer of arranged employment or is a skilled worker who has at least one year of experience in a designated occupation.

If the application is eligible for processing, the applicant may qualify as a 'skilled worker'. A skilled worker must have at least one year of continuous full-time paid work experience of a managerial, professional, or technical nature The work experience also must have occurred within the last ten years.

The Canadian Experience Class provides opportunities for those who have worked in certain occupations in Canada for a period of one year, and pass English or French language thresholds. This class expedites these workers, or former workers, through the application process. The same is true of those who are nominated or selected by provinces: all provinces and most territories have their own immigration selection programs, which also give priority to their candidates.

For more information on business immigration to Canada, refer to Baker & McKenzie's *Canada Business Immigration Manual*, available through the firm's website.

Appropriate Interview Questions

When hiring both foreign and domestic employees, employers are restricted in questions they may pose to potential applicants regarding their immigration status. Provincial human rights commissions release guidelines to assist employers in conducting a thorough and fair recruitment process. The Ontario Human Rights Commission makes the following recommendations to employers screening an applicant:

- Job advertising should not contain questions about race, ancestry, place of origin, colour, age, ethnic origin, citizenship, creed, sex, sexual orientation, record of offences, age, marital status, family status or handicap.
- Questions as to citizenship should be limited to asking if the applicant is legally entitled to work in Canada. Questions about a applicant's birthplace, ancestry, spouse or other relatives, Canadian citizenship, immigration status, experience in Canada, membership in Anglo-Canadian organizations, and any requests for proof of Canadian citizenship or a SIN are prohibited.
- As the number on the Social Insurance Card can provide information as to an applicant's immigration status, a request for a SIN may be made following a conditional offer of employment.

14.3. Obligation of Employer to Enforce Immigration Laws

Employers have a responsibility to ensure that employees have SINs and that those SINs permit the worker to work for that employer. There is no statutory provision requiring an employer to research employee backgrounds to verify their citizenship. However, if the employer fails to act upon learning that an employee is neither a citizen nor a permanent resident and without work authorization, the employer may be found guilty of committing an offence. It is recommended that the employer, if on notice that an employee or potential employee is not authorized to work in Canada, make inquiries. However, the employer should ensure that any inquiries as to a person's citizenship focus on eligibility to work in Canada and do not contravene human rights legislation.

Strict new compliance measures for employers of temporary foreign workers in force as of 1 January 2014 impose extensive record-keeping requirements and severe penalties for violation of the requirements of the program. Employers should seek legal advice on compliance.

14.4. Fines and Penalties

Both employers and employees who breach the IRPA are liable upon conviction of fines of up to USD 50,000 and imprisonment of up to two years. IRPA also prohibits those who knowingly counsel, induce, aid or abet in misrepresentation or withholding of material facts under the Act, which can impact both employees and employers. Fines for such violations are up to USD 100,000, with imprisonment of up to five years. There are also other forms of sanction available under the legislation, such as a six month bar on the ability of the worker to obtain another work permit. Inadmissibility can also result from violations of immigration law.

As of 1 January 2014 a new set of penalties has been introduced for employers who breach the requirements of the temporary foreign worker program. Penalties can now include public blacklisting of employers, bars on hiring foreign workers for two years, revocation of LMOs and work permits, fines and imprisonment for company executives and more.

14.5. Secondment/Foreign Assignment

Currently, there is no Canadian legislation providing guidance to employers sending employees overseas. However, there are several issues the employer should consider:

- The employer should know the role the employee will fulfil abroad. The employer should determine the date the employee will begin work in the foreign location and the end date for employment. The employer should draft a job description of the employee's foreign assignment for immigration purposes.
- The employer should learn about the employee's family obligations and other possible ramifications the assignment may have on the employee's personal life.
- The employer should have a sense of the employee's expectations and goals during his or her foreign assignment. These goals should align with the purpose for which the employer is sending the employee.
- The employer should contact an immigration lawyer to determine the steps to be taken for the employee to begin work.
- The employer should consult a tax specialist to assist the employer and employee with filing a foreign tax return.
- The employer should determine the compensation and benefits the employee will receive.
- The employer should draft the employment contract for the employee.

14.6. Checklist of Do's and Don'ts

- Do ask job applicants if they are entitled to work in Canada.
- Do follow up on any suspicion that an employee is not entitled to work in Canada.
- Do not ask questions that would violate applicable human rights legislation when interviewing a job applicant.
- Do plan ahead prior to sending employees across international borders.
- Do consider compensation, benefits, tax and contractual issues when sending an employee on secondment.

15. RESTRICTIVE COVENANTS AND PROTECTION OF TRADE SECRETS AND CONFIDENTIAL INFORMATION

15.1. Overview

Restrictive covenants are used by employers to restrain the current and post-employment activities of an employee. Similarly, the protection of trade secrets protects employers from losing their competitive edge by restricting an employee's ability to divulge certain information obtained throughout the course of employment. Some examples of confidential information include computer programmes, lists of suppliers, lists of customers and their specific needs, manufacturing process instructions, inventions and trade secretes, and lists of employees. Generally, in order for material to be considered a trade secret or confidential information, the material must have an indicia of secrecy and must provide the employer with an advantage over its competitors.

15.2. The Law of Trade Secrets

Courts define a trade secret as a plan, process, tool, mechanism or compound known only to its owner and those employees to whom it is necessary to confide it. A trade secret may consist of any formula, pattern, device or compilation of information which is used for one's business and gives the employer the opportunity to obtain an advantage over competitors who do not have such information. In determining the existence of a trade secret, courts will consider a variety of factors, including the nature of the employment and the employee's regular involvement with confidential material; the nature of the material itself; whether the employer has emphasized the confidential nature of the information to the employee; whether the material can be separated from non-confidential material;

whether the material affords the employer a competitive advantage over its competitors; the industry's general treatment of that particular type of information; and whether the information can be categorized as 'pure and applied' research, such as a novel invention.

Employees have an implied duty of fidelity restricting the employee's ability to appropriate his employer's trade secrets for his or her own benefit. This duty exists during the employment relationship and after the relationship has ended. While the common law permits employees to compete with former employers after the employment contract has ended, such competition must be fair. In determining the scope of the employee's right to compete, courts balance the employee's interest and right to exploit the general knowledge, expertise and skills that he or she has acquired throughout the course of employment; the employer's interest in exploiting its investment in the business; and the public interest in labour mobility and free competition. To overcome the courts' varying interpretation of 'fairness,' employers are encouraged to negotiate express provisions in the employment contract to prevent 'unfair' competition.

15.3. Restrictive Covenants and Non-compete Agreements

A restrictive covenant is an express contractual term prohibiting a current or future employee from exploiting the employer's trade secrets and trade connections with its customers, suppliers and employees. They are typically found in technical, professional, sales and managerial employee contracts. There are two types of restrictive covenants: (1) a non-competition clause, which prevents the employee from conducting business in competition to the former employer; and (2) a non-solicitation clause, which prohibits the former employee from soliciting the former employer's clients and customers or enticing employees to leave the former employer's client and customers to join the former employee's new business.

Traditionally, courts have been willing to enforce a narrowly drafted restrictive covenant which prohibits an employee from soliciting the employer's customers and clients or from exploiting confidential material obtained during the course of employment, but permits the employee to continue working in competition with the former employer. Broader non-competition clauses precluding an employee from engaging in any form of work that competes with the former employer's business are less likely to be enforced. If a non-competition clause is utilized, it must be restricted to a specified time period and constrained geographical space.

A restrictive covenant limiting geographical space must be in the public's interest to be enforced. For example, the Ontario High Court struck down a restrictive covenant which barred an obstetrician from practicing any form of medicine within five miles of St. Catharines. This was contrary to the public interest because there was a shortage of obstetricians in the area. In contrast, the British Columbia Supreme Court upheld a restrictive covenant that prevented a former manager from managing another pharmacy within a 25 mile radius of his former employer. The court determined that, given the number of accessible pharmacies within the 25 mile radius and the fact that the distance would not prevent loyal customers from following the manager, the covenant was not contrary to the public's interest.

A restrictive covenant is void as a restraint of trade unless the party seeking to enforce the covenant satisfies three factors. First, the employer must prove that it has a legitimate proprietary interest deserving protection. Second, the employer must prove that the restrictive covenant is reasonable. Reasonableness will be assessed through the duration and geographical restrictions and the overall effect the restriction has on both parties. Third, the restrictive covenant cannot be contrary to public interest. A restrictive covenant may be contrary to public interest if it violates statutory or common law, is injurious to the state or justice system, involves immorality and/or places an undue restraint on trade.

15.4. Checklist of Do's and Don'ts

- Do determine whether the information imparted to employees is confidential.
- Do stipulate which information is a trade secret.
- Do negotiate express restrictive covenants and trade secret clauses in the contract of employment.
- Do determine what is the most narrow geographical scope and time period required to ensure enforceability of the restrictive covenant.
- Do not draft a restrictive covenant that would be an unfair restraint on trade.

16. PROTECTION OF WHISTLEBLOWING CLAIMS

16.1. Overview

An exception to the duty of fidelity obligations is whistleblowing. Whistleblowing has been defined as the disclosure by current or former employees of illegal, immoral or illegitimate practices under the control of their employers, to persons or organizations that may be able to affect action. The wrongdoing must affect persons outside of the organization. An employee may divulge confidential information to prevent or rectify a wrong committed by the employer. Whistleblowing is permitted where the public's interest in the information outweighs the employer's right to confidentiality. Although the issue has not been thoroughly addressed in Canadian jurisprudence, certain situations clearly will afford the employee protection if he or she divulges confidential information against the employer. For example, the exception likely extends to the employer's criminal conduct, health and safety violations, human rights abuses, corruption within public organizations, tax fraud, or deliberate deception of the public.

Currently, there is very limited whistleblower protection in legislation. While Manitoba has a whistleblower protection act, it is limited to acts in or relating to public service. At the federal level, two acts protect whistleblowers; however, the protection is limited to the narrow subjects of the legislations – privacy and competition. In New Brunswick, protection may be found under section 28 of the *Employment Standards Act*. This provision protects against employment reprisals for employees who make complaints against their employers for the alleged violation of any provincial or federal legislation.

In the employment context, it is unlikely that an employer could show just cause for termination if it terminated an employee for whistleblowing, provided the employee acted in good faith and exhausted the appropriate internal mechanisms.

16.2. Checklist of Do's and Don'ts

- Do consider creating internal procedures that whistleblowers can use.
- Do investigate whistleblower allegations.
- Don't engage in reprisals against whistleblowers.

17. PROHIBITION OF DISCRIMINATION IN THE WORKPLACE

17.1. Overview of Anti-discrimination Laws

Discrimination is one of the fastest changing areas of employment law in Canada. In recent years, Canada's appellate courts have been called upon to rule on issues such as whether mandatory drug testing in employment relationships is permissible; whether government benefits that refuse to recognize same sex relationships are legal; and whether women are entitled to disability insurance benefits during normal pregnancies. Jurisdiction over employment law, including human rights laws, generally lies with each province. The federal government has authority over industries of national significance, such as atomic energy, telecommunication, banking, broadcasting, airlines, and inter-provincial transportation and shipping.

All Canadian provinces have detailed human rights legislation designed to protect employees from discrimination in employment on various grounds. Generally, most provincial human rights statutes prohibit discrimination on the basis of race, colour, ancestry, place of origin, ethnic origin or citizenship, creed, sex, sexual orientation, age, record of offences, marital or family status and handicap or disability, although the grounds vary by jurisdiction.

Where a person believes he or she has been a victim of discrimination, the person has the right to file a complaint with a provincial or federal administrative agency called a Human Rights Commission, or in some provinces, a Human Rights Tribunal.

Companies facing complaints of alleged discrimination may choose to rely on a bona fide occupational requirement or qualification to justify allegedly discriminatory standards, policies or practices. The Supreme Court of Canada has established a three step test an employer must satisfy to show that an otherwise discriminatory standard, factor, requirement or rule is bona fide and permissible. The employer must establish, on a balance of probabilities, that the standard, factor, requirement or rule: (a) was adopted for a purpose or goal that is rationally connected to the function being performed; (b) was adopted in good faith, in the belief that it is necessary for the fulfilment of the purpose or goal; and (c) is reasonably necessary to accomplish its purpose or goal, in the sense that it is impossible to accommodate the claimant without undue hardship. If this test is satisfied, the standard, factor, requirement or rule will be considered a bona fide occupation requirement or qualification.

17.2. Age Discrimination

Typically 'age' is defined as over the age of 18. Age discrimination is a growing issue in Canada as a result of changing workforce demographics. Canadian labour laws do not specify a mandatory retirement age for employees. In principle, older people have the right to be offered the same opportunities in employment, promotion and training as all other workers. Employers cannot refuse to hire, train or promote people simply because they are older.

Generally, federal and provincial human rights legislation finds the practice of mandatory retirement discriminatory. In certain jurisdictions, the human rights legislation does not consider it discriminatory to terminate employment because of the terms or conditions of a bona fide retirement or pension plan. If there is no such plan, employees who are forced to retire can file a complaint for age discrimination under the human rights legislation.

Under provincial human rights law, there is no discrimination when there are bona fide and reasonable requirements for an employment or occupation. For example, employees can maintain a mandatory retirement policy for certain workers if they can prove that the policy is reasonably connected to the job function; the mandatory retirement policy is applied in the honest belief that it is necessary for legitimate work-related purposes, such as safety concerns; and the policy is reasonably necessary to accomplish the legitimate work-related purposes, even with accommodation of the mature worker to the point of the employer's undue hardship.

17.3. Race Discrimination

Race is a prohibited ground of discrimination in all provincial and federal human rights codes. In Ontario, for example, the *Human Rights Code* states that every person has a right to equal treatment with respect to employment without discrimination because of race. The Ontario Human Rights Commission defines racial harassment as treating someone unfairly because of race, colour or ancestry.

17.4. Sex Discrimination/Sexual Harassment

In Canada, all employees have a legally protected right to work in an environment where their dignity is respected and they are free of harassment. This protection is based on provincial and federal human rights legislation. Most employees are subject to the human rights laws of the province in which they reside and work. However, employers who work in those sectors that fall within federal jurisdiction, such as banking, telecommunications, airlines, and railroads, are protected by the federal *Canadian Human Rights Act*.

Sexual harassment is prohibited by statute and by the anti-discrimination provisions of the various human rights laws. Most provinces, including Ontario and Quebec, have specifically provided in their human rights statutes that sexual harassment in the workplace is a human rights violation. For example, the Ontario *Human Rights Code* provides that every employee has a right to freedom from sexual harassment in the workplace by the employer, an agent of the employer or by another employee. The *Code* also states that every person has a right to be free from:

(i) Sexual solicitation or advances made by a person in a position to confer, grant, or deny a benefit or advancement to the person, where the person making the solicitation or advance knows of reasonably ought to know that it is unwelcome; or

(ii) A reprisal or a threat of reprisal for the rejection of a sexual solicitation or advance, where the reprisal is made or threatened by a person in a position to confer, grant, or deny a benefit or advancement to the person.

In those jurisdictions where the statute does not contain a specific prohibition against sexual harassment, employees still are protected against sexual harassment by the provinces in each jurisdiction that prohibit sex discrimination in the workplace. Courts and tribunals in Canada uniformly have found sexual harassment to be a form of sex discrimination. In addition, Canadian courts and tribunals have been guided by certain statutory definitions of sexual harassment. For example, the *Canada Labour Code* defines sexual harassment as any conduct, comment, gesture, or contact of a sexual nature that: (a) is likely to cause offence or humiliation to any employee; or (b) might, on reasonable grounds, be perceived by that employee as placing a condition of a sexual nature on employment or on any opportunity for training or promotion.

Certain provinces protect against discrimination on the basis of gender identity or gender expression. In many other provinces, Human Rights Tribunals also held that transgender persons would be protected under the definition of 'sex' and 'disability'.

17.5. Handicap and Disability Discrimination

Human rights legislation generally defines disability broadly. In Ontario disability is defined as:

(a) any degree of physical disability, infirmity, malformation or disfigurement that is caused by bodily injury, birth defect or illness, including diabetes mellitus, epilepsy, a brain injury, any degree of paralysis, amputation, lack of physical co-ordination, blindness or visual impediment, deafness or hearing impediment, muteness or speech impediment, or physical reliance on a guide dog or other animal or on a wheelchair or other remedial appliance or device;

(b) a condition of mental impairment or a developmental disability;

(c) a learning disability, or a dysfunction in one or more of the processes involved in understanding or using symbols or spoken language;

(d) a mental disorder; or

(e) an injury or disability for which benefits were claimed or received under the insurance plan established under the Workplace Safety and Insurance Act, 1997.

Both physical and mental disabilities are included as prohibited grounds of discrimination.

A wide variety of impairments have been classified as a disability or handicap, including: bipolar disorder, alcoholism, drug dependency, tobacco addiction, insomnia, chronic fatigue syndrome, fear of flying and obsessive compulsive disorder. To constitute a disability, the employee's condition must possess a measure of severity, permanence and persistence.

The laws provide that employers may discriminate when the individual in question cannot perform the essential duties of the position in question. This analysis applies to all protected categories, but most of the jurisprudence has developed from disability cases. The employer must show that it attempted to accommodate the individual's disability to the point of undue hardship. For example, section 17(1) of the Ontario Human Rights Code states that the right of a person under the Code is not infringed if the person is incapable of performing or fulfilling the essential duties or requirements attending the exercise of the right because of disability. This type of defence is called a bona fide occupational requirement. It permits discrimination where the requirement is necessary for the performance of the job, and the individual cannot do the job because he or she cannot perform the bona fide occupation requirement. Courts generally have held that to successfully rely on a bona fide occupational requirement defence, an employer must prove it implemented the bona fide occupational requirement in good faith and that the requirement was necessary for the efficient and economical performance of the job without endangering the employee being accommodated, other employees, or the general public.

The employer's duty to accommodate the employee is a statutory requirement. For example, section 17(2) of the Ontario Code stipulates that no tribunal or court shall find a person incapable unless it is satisfied that the needs of the person cannot be accommodated without undue hardship on the person responsible for accommodating those needs, considering the cost, outside sources of funding, if any, and health and safety requirements.

17.6. National Origin Discrimination

National origin is a prohibited ground of discrimination in all provincial human rights legislation. National origin is not defined in the legislation, but it has been interpreted by human rights tribunals as the denial of equal treatment because of an individual's place of origin or because an individual has the physical, cultural or linguistic characteristics of a national origin group. Tribunals have found discrimination on the basis of national origin in several instances. In one case, the British Columbia Human Rights Tribunal found discrimination where an employee was denied a job at a lumber mill because he was not perfectly fluent in English. Although he could read English and could speak it to a certain degree, Punjabi was his first language. In another case, a teacher from Iran was unable to provide original documents attesting to her qualifications. The Ontario Divisional Court held that the selection committee's practices amounted to discrimination on the basis of place of origin. The factors courts consider to determine the existence of racial discrimination can be applied to discrimination on the basis of national origin. These factors may include past hiring and firing decisions, evidence of discrimination patterns against one or more groups, and evidence of a discriminatory environment through slurs and comments.

17.7. Religious Discrimination

Employers may not discriminate against employees on the basis of religion. Religious discrimination can be found where an employee is required to work on certain days of the week contrary to his or her religion, where an employee is forbidden from wearing a religious form of dress or article of clothing during the course of employment, or where employees are permitted to take religious holidays but are not given pay.

17.8. Military Status Discrimination

Military status is not a ground for discrimination in Canada.

17.9. Pregnancy Discrimination

The Supreme Court of Canada held that pregnancy is included in the definition of 'sex'. Therefore, refusal to hire an application because she is pregnant or to reasonably accommodate her in the workplace due to pregnancy is unlawful. 'Sex' also has been interpreted to include illnesses, medical complications such as miscarriage and surgery related to child birth.

17.10. Marital Status Discrimination

Marital status discrimination arises when an employee is penalized because he or she is or is not married. Examples of martial status discrimination include policies precluding spouses of current employees from applying for a job, differential travel and relocation allowances based on marital status, and pension plans that deny survivor benefits to a spouse unless the employee dies after retirement.

The definition of marital status varies slightly in each province. In Ontario, martial status is defined as the status of being married, single, widowed, divorced or separated and includes the status of living with a person in a conjugal relationship outside marriage.

17.11. Sexual Orientation Discrimination

Discrimination on the basis of sexual orientation is included in every provinces' human rights legislation.

17.12. Retaliation

Many employers have policies in place which protect a complainant who has brought a human rights complaint from facing retaliation. In addition to internal policies, provincial statutes also protect a complainant from reprisal. For example, the British Columbia code states that a person must not evict, discharge, suspend, expel, intimidate, coerce, impose any pecuniary or other penalty on, deny a right or benefit to or otherwise discriminate against a person because that person complains or is named in a complaint, gives evidence or otherwise assists in a complaint or other proceeding under the *Code*.

17.13. Constructive Dismissal

Constructive discharge or dismissal occurs where the employer has not directly fired the employee, but rather has failed to comply with the contract of employment in a major respect. The employer must unilaterally and materially change the terms of employment, forcing the employee to quit. The employee can sue for constructive dismissal just as he or she would for wrongful dismissal, even though it is the employee who ended the relationship. If the degree of discrimination encountered on the job is severe, the employee can treat his or her contract as effectively terminated. The

British Columbia Human Rights Tribunal found constructive dismissal where an employee, a Jehovah's Witness, refused to take part in putting up Christmas decorations (artificial poinsettias) at his employer's store. The employer insisted he do so or leave. The Tribunal ruled that the employer made no attempt to accommodate the complainant's religious beliefs. The ruling is an indication that employers will not be able to use a 'just cause' defence for constructive dismissal if they cannot show that they attempted to accommodate their employees' to the point of undue hardship.

17.14. Checklist of Do's and Don'ts

- Do be aware of prohibited grounds of discrimination.
- Do attempt to accommodate the employee's disability or other prohibited ground of discrimination to the point of undue hardship.
- Do initiate policies that are not discriminatory.
- Do train managers and other employees on appropriate workplace behaviour.
- Do require that the employee be an active participant in the accommodation process.

18. SMOKING IN THE WORKPLACE

18.1. Overview

All provinces have enacted smoke-free workplace legislation. These statutes require employers to prohibit their employees and visitors from smoking on the premises. The *Smoke-Free Ontario Act* prohibits smoking in all 'enclosed workplaces', which includes the inside of any building or roofed vehicle that employees work in or have access to during the course of employment.

The employer faces specific obligations to ensure the workplace is kept smoke free. Under the *Smoke-Free Ontario Act*, these obligations include ensuring that: no one smokes in the workplace, prescribed 'no smoking' signs are displayed, notice is given to every worker that smoking is prohibited in enclosed spaces, and workers and visitors to the workplace who refuse to comply are removed from the workplace.

A breach of the smoke-free work place act is punishable by fine. In Ontario, the maximum fine for an individual offender is CAD 4,000 for the first offence, CAD 10,000 for a second offence, CAD 20,000 for a third offence and CAD 100,000 for any further offences. For a corporate offender, the fines are CAD 10,000 for the first offence, CAD 20,000 for the second offence, CAD 50,000 for the third offence and CAD 150,000 for any further offences.

Municipalities are able to pass stricter smoke-free by-laws as necessary.

18.2. Checklist of Do's and Don'ts

- Do ensure that employees, contractors, and visitors do not smoke in the workplace.
- Do ensure that the prescribed no-smoking signs are posted.
- Do ensure that ashtrays are not available.
- Do ensure that notice is given to every employee that smoking is prohibited.
- Do ensure that workers and visitors that do not comply with the anti-smoking rules are removed from the workplace.

19. USE OF DRUGS AND ALCOHOL IN THE WORKPLACE

19.1. Overview

An employee's inadequate job performance over an extended period resulting from drug/alcohol abuse can support dismissal for a cause of the employee. Courts, however, balance the adverse effects of alcohol and drug use on the employee's health, safety and job performance against the requirement that employees not be discriminated against on the basis of a prohibited ground of discrimination. Consequently, prior to dismissing the employee, the employer should verify whether or not the employee suffers from an alcohol or drug related disability. Since alcoholism and drug addiction are considered to be disabilities under human rights legislation, the employer is under an obligation to reasonably accommodate the employee's illness to the point of undue hardship. Reasonable accommodation may include involving the employee in rehabilitation programmes and asking the employee about his or her conduct.

In a recent policy statement, the Ontario Human Rights Commission stated that drug and alcohol testing is a prima facie violation of human rights legislation. However, an employer may justify discriminatory rules if it satisfies three criteria: (1) the employer adopted the policy or standard for a purpose rationally connected to the performance of the job; (2) the employer adopted the particular policy or standard in an honest and good faith belief that it was necessary to the fulfilment of that legitimate, work-related purpose; and (3) the policy or standard is reasonably necessary to the accomplishment of the legitimate, work-related purpose. This last element requires the employer to demonstrate that it is impossible to accommodate individual employees without imposing undue hardship on the employer.

Several principles have emerged from cases in the past two decades regarding drug and alcohol testing. In 2000, the Ontario Court of Appeal ruled that an employer cannot administer a compulsory drug test to all or to randomly selected job applicants prior to an offer of employment because urinalysis and other current methods of conducting drug testing cannot reliably predict that an employee will be impaired while performing his or her job. The Ontario Court of Appeal also held that once an employee has been hired, random drug testing remains illegal because of its inability to predict current or future job impairment. However, the Court of Appeal has recognized that random alcohol testing is permissible under certain conditions. For example, random breathalyzer tests are acceptable where there is no practical alternative to supervise an employee's alcohol consumption while on the job. The Court of Appeal ruled that random alcohol testing is justified only in certain circumstances, including in the context of safety-sensitive positions, where the safety of other employees and/or the general public would be at risk. The same judgment also held that mandatory drug and alcohol testing of current employees is permissible where there is reliable evidence that employees are impaired while on the job. Finally, policies that require employees in safety-sensitive positions to proactively disclose current substance abuse problems, as well as past problems for alcohol or drugs (within the last five or six years for alcohol dependency and six years for drug dependency, the point where the risk of relapse is no greater than the risk a member of the general population will suffer a substance abuse problem) are permissible in certain circumstances

Social host liability frequently is applied to employers who permit or provide alcohol at company sponsored events. Indeed, an employer who supplies alcohol to its employees owes a greater duty than a host owes to invited guests. If an employee becomes intoxicated and injures him/herself or others, the employer may be found liable for events that occur after the employee has left the company sponsored event. As a result, employers should pay greater attention to workplace alcohol policies and be vigilant at events where alcohol is supplied.

19.2. Checklist of Do's and Don'ts

- Do determine if an employee's drug or alcohol use would qualify as a disability under human rights legislation.
- Do not administer compulsory drug tests to job applicants or employees.

- Do administer mandatory drug or alcohol tests if there is reasonable suspicion that an employee is impaired.
- Do not extend compulsory disclosure of past drug or alcohol use beyond what is necessary.
- Don't turn a blind eye to intoxication at company events.

20. AIDS, HIV, SARS, BLOODBORNE PATHOGENS

20.1. Overview

According to Canadian jurisprudence, AIDS and its precursor, HIV, are included in the definition of disability under Canadian human rights legislation. The Ontario Human Rights Commission has stated that those living with HIV/AIDS should be free from all forms of discrimination. As a result, an employer must accommodate an employee living with HIV/AIDS unless there is a bona fide occupational requirement which would prevent the employee from fulfilling the terms and conditions of employment.

Medical tests conducted prior to the offer of employment and administered to all individuals or to randomly selected individuals in order to eliminate those suffering from a protected disability are unlawful. Any medical assessments of a person's ability to fulfil employment obligations may only be conducted after a conditional offer of employment. If a medical test discloses that the conditionally accepted applicant is unable to perform the job as required, the employer may refuse a final offer of employment if there is a bona fide occupational requirement that the applicant cannot fulfil and the employer made efforts to reasonably accommodate the disability to the point of undue hardship.

SARS and other blood borne pathogens are listed as reportable communicable diseases under provincial regulations. In the event that a communicable disease is introduced into the workplace, the employer should remove the employee from the workplace and ensure that he or she receives proper medical assessment and treatment. As a corollary to such treatment by the attending physician, the medical care provider is required to disclose the incident to the provincial Ministry of Health. This information then will be communicated by the Ministry to the federal health authority that officially records and monitors potential health crises. The employer should conduct a consultation with the employee and the attending physician regarding the required report to the Ministry and arrange a follow up consultation with the Ministry pursuant to such reporting.

The employer should confirm that workplace safety protocols were and continue to be followed and should only allow the infected employee to return to work upon receipt of a medical certificate or evidence of non-infection. All potentially exposed co-workers should be notified of the incident. Such notification should be discreet and individual. The notification should outline the risk of exposure associated with the disease and self-assessment guidelines. In disclosing an employee's communicable disease to the Ministry of Health and to co-workers, an appropriate balance must be struck between the employee's right to privacy and the public's interest in safety.

Employment standards legislation in most provinces and at the federal level provide for protected sick leave. Further, human rights legislation prohibits termination of employment solely on the fact that an employee was unable to work for a short period of time due to an illness or disease that qualifies as a disability due to its chronic nature.

20.2. Checklist of Do's and Don'ts

- Do treat an employee living with HIV/AIDS as a person with a disability.
- Do accommodate the employee's disability.
- Do not terminate the employment of the employee or fail to hire the applicant with the disability unless accommodation is not possible without undue hardship.
- Do not terminate the disabled applicant or employee unless there is a bona fide occupational requirement that he or she cannot fulfil.
- Do notify the Ministry of Health of any incidents of communicable diseases.
- Do provide the employee with protected, unpaid leave during the course of his or her illness.
- Do notify co-workers of potential exposure.

21. DRESS AND GROOMING REQUIREMENTS

21.1. Overview

Dress code policies are left to the individual employer to determine. However, courts have ruled on clothing policies when religious and safety concerns have been at issue. In one case, an employer transferred a Sikh employee from the mill floor to an outside driving position because he could not remove his turban to wear to a mandated breathing apparatus. The British Columbia Human Rights Tribunal held that the employer did not discriminate against the employee. The employer's dress code policy was justified because his inability to wear the apparatus posed a potential safety hazard to the employee and his co-workers. The fact that there was no alternate breathing apparatus that could fit over the turban demonstrated that the employer could not reasonably accommodate the employee's religious attire. If employee's religious attire may be accommodated safely or with minimal risk and there is no undue hardship imposed on the employer, then the religious attire should be permitted in the workplace.

Dress codes have received greater attention in the unionized environment where such issues can be bargained over and employees can bring grievances against the employer. In the non-union environment, such policies are left to the employer and the courts will not intervene unless there is a human rights issue or a breach of an employment contract. In the union context, employers can implement employee dress codes.

So long as the dress code is reasonable and serves legitimate business and safety objectives. An arbitration board in Manitoba listed three key factors decision makers will consider when determining if a dress code is reasonable – the dress code rules must relate to a legitimate business purpose, be reasonably related to contemporary community standards and not unduly or unnecessarily impinge upon the employee's personal rights, and consistently enforced. The employer's own verbal opinion as to why a dress code is reasonable is insufficient.

21.2. Checklist of Do's and Don'ts

- Do accommodate religious attire to the greatest extent possible.
- Do ensure that safety is considered paramount to other considerations.
- Do determine if the safety of the employee who is requesting accommodation would only be minimally affected.
- Do ensure that dress codes are reasonable and necessary.

22. PRIVACY, TECHNOLOGY AND TRANSFER OF PERSONAL DATA

22.1. Privacy Rights of Employees

Employee privacy is legislatively protected for federal employees and employees in provinces with privacy legislation. Most provinces, however, do not have comprehensive legislated safeguards for the privacy of employees in the private sector. To date, only Quebec, British Columbia, and Alberta have legislation governing privacy rights in the employment relationship. Manitoba has passed privacy legislation which is not yet in force. Significantly, recent judicial interpretations of these statutes show a movement toward recognition of a tort of breach of privacy. The Ontario Court of Appeal has expressly recognized a tort relating to invasion of privacy. It is expected that Courts of other provinces will follow suit. The nature and degree of privacy to which a person is entitled is that which is reasonable under the circumstances, giving due regard to the lawful interests of others. In determining whether one's privacy has been violated, regard must be given to the nature, incidence and occasion of the act or conduct and to the nature of the relationship between the parties. An employee's claim for invasion of privacy was successful in one British Columbia case, where a retail chain breached the employee's privacy rights by using his name and photograph in advertisements without his permission five weeks after his termination. The case suggests that employees have a right to control the manner in which employers use their personal information.

For the provinces that have enacted privacy legislation restrictions on the collection, storage, use and disclosure of personal information are extended to include electronic surveillance of employees. Other provinces without privacy acts are governed by the common law. The Ontario Superior Court of Justice addressed the reasonableness of electronic surveillance in a case involving the secret installation of a video camera in an employee's office without her knowledge. The employer installed the camera in the complainant's office based on the suspicion that unidentified employees were stealing. The court found that the employer's reasons for installing the camera did not justify the gross invasion of privacy the complainant experienced. The work atmosphere had become poisoned to such an extent that the employee was entitled to refuse to work.

The employer must adduce hard evidence to show that the activity warranting electronic surveillance is sufficiently serious and not mere speculation. In addition, the employer must show that it has exhausted all other less intrusive means of combating the alleged illegal activity.

22.2. Checklist of Do's and Don'ts

- Do protect employee's personal information.
- Do not disclose employee information unless it is for an identified purpose.
- Do collect employees' personal information for business purposes only.
- Do not subject workers to electronic surveillance unless there is hard evidence to necessitate its use.
- Do be aware that an employee may have an action in tort for invasion of privacy if personal information is used without his or her permission.

23. WORKPLACE INVESTIGATIONS

23.1. Overview

There are a variety of workplace incidents that may warrant investigation, including complaints of discrimination, harassment, fraud, theft and whistleblowing. There are several factors an employer should consider to ensure a fair investigation of workplace incidents, including the nature of the incident, whether the incident occurred during or after work hours, whether it may be criminal, and the potential for human rights breaches. These factors may affect the manner in which the employer conducts the investigation. If the employee is unionized, the collective agreement should be consulted to determine if any investigative provisions are in effect. An employer has a positive duty to investigate workplace incidents, particularly where an employee alleges a contravention of a human rights code.

The investigation process used by the employer will depend on the nature of the allegation. An investigation typically includes interviewing those involved in the incident or who witnessed the incident; collecting evidence that may provide insight into the incident, such as time cards, e-mails, accounting or inventory records, invoices or sales documentation, or building access records; and taking photographs of actual evidence, such as damaged or stolen property. Interviews should be conducted soon after the alleged incident occurred or the employer was made aware of the need for an investigation. Collective agreements should be consulted to determine any procedural protocol for interviewing employees, especially in regard to union representation. If there is a chance that the incident may be criminal in nature, the employer should receive legal advice before conducting any interviews.

An employer's right to search an employee's person or personal effects must be balanced with the employee's right to privacy. Arbitrators have held that the unionized employer should not be able to conduct a search of an employee's personal effects unless there is a real and substantial suspicion of wrongdoing. The employer also must establish that adequate cause to justify the search existed, that available alternatives were exhausted, that reasonable steps were taken to inform the employee and that the search was conducted in a systematic and non-discriminatory manner.

23.2. Checklist of Do's and Don'ts

- Do determine whether or not a collective agreement governs investigations of workplace incidents.

- Do follow protocol detailed in the collective agreement if one is in place.
- Do tailor the investigation process based on the nature of the allegation.
- Do balance the employer's right to search with the employee's right to privacy.
- Do not use surveillance techniques unless the measure is reasonable in the circumstances.
- Do protect the confidentiality of employees launching whistleblowing claims.

24. AFFIRMATIVE ACTION/NONDISCRIMINATION REQUIREMENTS

24.1. Overview

Both federal and provincial jurisdictions have employment or pay equity legislation that requires an employer to consider equity and non-discriminatory requirements in the employment context.

Federal Employment Equity

The federal *Employment Equity Act* requires employers to meet thresholds for hiring applicants from protected groups. The Act applies to all federally-regulated employers with hundred or more employees, including private sector employers in industries such as banking, telecommunicating and international and interprovincial transportation.

The federal act requires that employers achieve employment equity by identifying and eliminating employment barriers against persons in designated groups. This is achieved by instituting policies and practices and making such reasonable accommodations as will ensure that persons in designated groups achieve a degree of representation in the employer's workforce that reflects their representation in either the Canadian workforce, or those segments of the Canadian workforce that are identifiable by qualification, eligibility or geography and from which the employer may reasonably be expected to draw employees. 'Designated groups' include women, aboriginal peoples, persons with disabilities and members of visible minorities. 'Visible minorities' are persons, other than aboriginal peoples, who are non-Caucasian in race or non-white in colour.

There are some limitations on the extent to which employers must recruit designated groups. The obligation to implement employment equity does not require an employer (a) to take a particular measure to implement employment equity where the taking of that measure would cause undue hardship; (b) to hire or promote persons who do not meet the essential qualifications for the work to be performed; (c) to create new positions in its workforce; or (d) to override seniority rights in implementing layoffs and recalls.

In achieving employment equity, an employer's first step is to collect information and conduct an analysis of its workforce in order to determine the degree of under representation of persons in designated groups in that workforce. The employer then must conduct a review of its employment systems, policies and practices to identify employment barriers against persons in designated groups resulting from those systems, policies and practices. Then, the employer must prepare an employment equity plan. The plan should specify: the positive policies and practices that the employer will use in the short-term for the hiring, training, promotion and retention of persons in designated groups; the measures to be taken by the employer to eliminate any employment barriers identified by the review; a timetable for the implementation of such measures and practices; short term numerical goals for the hiring and promotion of persons in designated groups; and the employer's long term goals for increasing the representation of persons in designated groups.

To ensure ongoing compliance, the employer should monitor the progress of the system and review and revise its plan to ensure that equity goals are being met. Records tracing the failure or success of the employment equity process also should be maintained. Finally, the employer must file an annual report with the Minister which includes comprehensive and detailed information about the workforce.

Provincial Employment Equity

Quebec and Ontario, have a Pay Equity Act that applies to private sector employers. The purpose of this legislation is to redress systemic gender discrimination in compensation for work performed by employees in female job classes. Pay equity is achieved when the job rate for the female job class is at least equal to the job rate for a male job class in the same workplace where the work performed in the two job classes is of equal or comparable value.

Employers with 10 or more employees in either Quebec or Ontario should have pay equity plans setting out: the method of comparison employers will use to determine the ratio of female-to-male representation in one job class; the results of such comparison; all positions and job classes in which differences in compensation are permitted and reasons for such differences; and how the compensation in female job classes will be adjusted to achieve pay equity. Aside from legislative requirements, provincially regulated employers are under an obligation to maintain a workplace free of discrimination.

24.2. Checklist of Do's and Don'ts

- Do actively recruit designated groups as employees.
- Do institute policies and practices to ensure that designated persons achieve representation in the workplace.
- Do ensure ongoing compliance.
- Do not implement employment equity policies if doing so would create undue hardship, result in hiring unqualified persons, result in hiring persons lacking merit, create new positions, or override seniority or recall rights.

25. RESOLUTION OF LABOUR, DISCRIMINATION AND EMPLOYMENT DISPUTES: LITIGATION, ARBITRATION, MEDIATION AND CONCILIATION

25.1. Internal Dispute Resolution Process

If employees are unionized, the collective agreement will contain a grievance procedure to resolve disputes between the employer and the union members. It is a statutory requirement that the employee exhaust any grievance procedures before commencing arbitration. The grievance procedure in a collective agreement typically involves multiple steps. Prior to hearing a grievance, the employee should have an informal discussion with the supervisor. This informal discussion phase allows the supervisor to hear the issues raised by the employee. It also provides an opportunity to resolve the issue prior to commencing the grievance process. During this meeting the supervisor should focus on collecting as many facts as possible about the employee's claim and creating a documentary record, including a completed investigation report, witness statements, the employee's file, previous incidents of similar cases, and the collective agreement.

If the dispute is not settled during the initial phase, then a grievance is filed. The formal process begins with the employee completing a grievance form provided by the union, outlining the facts of the grievance, the articles of the collective agreement allegedly violated, and the remedy sought. Upon receipt of the grievance, a senior representative of management must meet with the employee and the union representative within prescribed time limits to discuss the problem. If the employer's decision is not satisfactory, the grievance may then be transmitted to arbitration. To keep the process open and promote conflict resolution, nothing said during the course of the grievance procedure can be admitted at arbitration.

Recently, non-union employers have begun including dispute resolution processes to resolve employee complaints. The use of internal dispute resolution processes encourages non-adversarial resolution of issues. Recent studies, however, have shown that only one third of non-unionized Canadian workplaces offer internal grievance mechanisms. Canadian courts also have not addressed internal grievance procedures, suggesting that such procedures are not yet widespread in a non-unionized setting.

25.2. Mediation and Conciliation

In almost all dispute resolution mechanisms, mediation is part of the process. Some systems may make it mandatory, while in other instances it may be optional. Under the Ontario *Labour Relations Act*, the parties may bring the dispute to a mediator despite any grievance or arbitration provision in a collective agreement. The parties will submit the dispute to a neutral third party who is well educated in labour and employment issues. The mediator will not issue a judgment. Rather, his or her role is to assist the employer and employee in reaching a settlement. Anything discussed at mediation is confidential. Mediation often is sought following the internal dispute resolution process in an effort to settle disputes prior to arbitration.

25.3. Arbitration

It is a statutory requirement that all collective agreements contain arbitration clauses. Arbitrations lead to a final and binding settlement between the parties. In the case of a collective agreement, the arbitrator's decision binds all employers and employees affected by the decision. Arbitrations may be conducted by one impartial arbitrator or a panel of arbitrators.

The structure of an arbitration proceeding is similar to that of a court of law. Except in cases of termination or discipline, where the burden is always on the employer, the burden of proof rests with the party bringing the grievance to make a clear case that the other party violated the collective agreement.

Although labour arbitrators have thc jurisdiction to deal with human rights complaints issues arising out of the collective agreement, human rights complaints can alternatively be directed to the provincial human rights commission or tribunal. In most provinces, the human rights commission acts as a gatekeeper to the provincial human rights tribunal. Proceedings in front of the human rights tribunal are essentially arbitrations, although the parties do not select the panel members. In Ontario and British Columbia, the human rights commissions do not accept complaints of discrimination and applications complaining about discrimination are filed directly by the complainant with the tribunal. The human rights commissions of these two provinces have a variety of responsibilities, including promoting human rights dialogue, educating the public on its rights, conducting public inquiries, initiating their own applications, and intervening in human rights tribunal proceedings.

The use of formal processes like arbitration remains rare in non-unionized settings in Canada. If non-unionized employees agree on an arbitration clause, their right to seek redress through the regular court system is severely limited. Provincial arbitration acts show a preference for dismissing claims that are bound by arbitration agreements. For example, Ontario's *Arbitration Act, 1991* states that if a party commences a court proceeding for a matter that ought to be submitted to arbitration based on an arbitration agreement, the court shall stay the proceeding pending resolution of the matter at arbitration. The court can only refuse the stay under narrow exceptions. These include if a party entered into the arbitration agreement while under a legal incapacity, the arbitration agreement is invalid, the subject-matter of the dispute is not capable of being the subject of arbitration under Ontario law, the motion was brought with undue delay, or the matter is a proper one for default or summary judgment. The restrictions placed on the availability of court intervention may render arbitration undesirable for certain non-unionized parties.

25.4. Litigation

Litigation is costly and time consuming in comparison to other forms of dispute resolution, such as arbitration and mediation. Litigation may arise in the employment context through several instances, including wrongful and constructive dismissal.

Parties who are bound by a collective agreement are required to resolve their disputes through the arbitration process outlined in the collective agreement and will generally not be heard by a court. Should a party be dissatisfied with the arbitration decision, it can apply to have the decision judicially reviewed by the court. In most cases, however, the court will defer to the arbitrator's expertise and discretion, unless the decision was unreasonable or breaches the principles of fundamental justice.

The litigation process for non-unionized parties begins when the plaintiff (usually the employee or former employee) prepares a statement of claim containing a concise statement of the facts on which the plaintiff intends to rely. The plaintiff serves the statement of claim on all defendants and files an affidavit of service with the court. The defendant prepares a statement of defence, serves it on the plaintiff, and files a copy with the court together with proof of service. The defendant may counterclaim against the plaintiff, cross claim against a co-defendant, or make a third party claim against a non-party. If the defendant employer does not serve a statement of defence, the plaintiff may obtain a default judgment. Documents are exchanged, Examination for Discovery are conducted, and mediation is completed. If the parties still have not settled their dispute, the parties must then set the action down for trial. Either party may set the action down for trial by serving and filing the trial record. A trial record includes a copy of all pleadings and orders relating to the trial. Pre-trial conferences may occur at a party or the judge's initiative in an effort to settle the case or narrow the issues. If the matter proceeds to trial, the plaintiff and defendant will make opening statements, examine and cross-examine each other's witnesses, introduce exhibits, and make closing arguments. Finally, the court will render a decision in favour of the plaintiff or defendant.

25.5. Fines, Penalties and Damages

Employees whose complaints are upheld under human rights legislation may be awarded general damages for injury to dignity, for example, or special damages for demonstrable loss, such as loss of income. Human rights tribunals tend to adopt a 'make whole' approach when assessing the claimant's future employment prospects. Various factors are taken into account when assessing the claimant's damages, and the analysis is very fact specific. The Canadian Human Rights Tribunal has recognized that if the employee likely would have received a promotion if not for the discriminatory practice, then damages should include the wages the employee would have earned but for the wrongful conduct. Similarly, the British Columbia Human Rights Tribunal held that if the claimant would have been terminated due to economic reasons had he or she not been dismissed prematurely, the calculation for damages should include only wages up to that point in time at which the employee likely would have been terminated to avoid unjust enrichment. If it is unlikely that the employee would have been able to mitigate his damages by finding a replacement job, lost wages should be calculated up to the time at which the employee would have retired. Damages awarded for successful human rights claims are dependent on the facts of each case and thus vary widely.

In the context of wrongful dismissal civil litigation claims, the Supreme Court of Canada enunciated four factors to determine the length of reasonable notice that should be given to terminated employees. These factors include: the character of the employment, the length of service of the employee, the age of the employee, and the availability of similar employment considering the experience, training and qualifications of the employee. Finally, damages may be awarded for the manner in which the employee was dismissed where the employee can prove actual damages.

Parties who are found by an employment standards officer to have contravened the provincial employment standards acts are liable to pay fines or face possible imprisonment. For example, section 132 of the Ontario *Employment Standards Act* states a person who contravenes this Act is guilty of an offence and on conviction is liable, if the person is an individual, to a fine of not more than CAD 50,000 or to imprisonment for a term of not more than twelve months or to both. If the guilty party is a corporation, it will be subject to a fine of not more than CAD 100,000. If the corporation has previously been convicted of an offence under the Act, it will be subject to a fine of not more than CAD 250,000. However, if the corporation has more than one previous conviction, it will face a fine of not more than CAD 500,000. Imprisonment is exceedingly rare and is used in only the most egregious circumstances.

25.6. Checklist of Do's and Don'ts

- Do following the grievance process contained in the collective agreement.
- Do attempt to resolve grievances informally before filing a formal grievance form with the employer.
- Do attempt to resolve grievances through mediation before resorting to arbitration.
- Do not bring a claim into the litigation system if the claim is one that is covered by an arbitration agreement or a collective agreement.
- Do consider all relevant factors when assessing damages under successful human rights violation complaints.
- Do consider all relevant factors when determining a proper notice period for wrongful dismissal claims.

26. EMPLOYER RECORDKEEPING, DATA PROTECTION, AND EMPLOYEE ACCESS TO PERSONNEL FILES AND RECORDS

26.1. Overview

As mentioned above, *PIPEDA* addresses how employers can use employee information in the federally-regulated private sector. Currently, only Alberta,

British Columbia and Quebec have passed legislation applying to private sector employment privacy issues. Manitoba has also passed such legislation through it is not yet in force. The purpose of these acts is to govern the collection, use and disclosure of personal information by organizations in a manner that recognizes both the right of individuals to protect their personal information and the need of organizations to collect, use or disclose personal information for purposes that a reasonable person would consider appropriate in the circumstances.

26.2. Personnel Files

Personnel files are required to be maintained and include information about the employee such as name, address, date of employment, and information regarding the hours worked, including overtime. Vacation entitlements, public holidays and other information about the employee's work also is included in the records. A significant portion of the employee's personnel records is required to be kept for up to six years by the employer for inspection by various government agencies.

An employer may not collect employee personal information without the consent of the employee unless the collection is for the purposes of establishing, managing or terminating an employment relationship between the organization and the individual or for another specifically enumerated purpose listed in the applicable privacy legislation. Prior to the organization collecting the employee personal information without the consent, the organization must notify an individual that it will be collecting employee personal information about the individual and the purposes for the collection.

26.3. Confidentiality Rules

The provincial acts permit the disclosure of personal employee information in certain circumstances. Generally, an employer may disclose personal employee information about an individual without consent if the individual is, or was, an employee of the organization or the disclosure of the information is for the purpose of recruiting a potential employee. An employer cannot disclose personal information about an individual without consent unless: the disclosure is reasonable for the purposes for which the information is being disclosed; the information consists only of information that is related to the employment or volunteer work relationship of the individual; and in the case of an individual who is an employee of the organization, the organization has, before disclosing the information, provided the individual with reasonable notification that the information is going to be disclosed and the purposes for the disclosure.

In addition to statutory requirements, employers should adhere to the following best practices: medical records should be separated from the personnel file; access to personal employee information should be limited to the appropriate persons; and personnel files should be kept in a locked area.

26.4. Employee Access

The provincial privacy acts places employers under a positive obligation to provide employees with access to their personal information. Quebec's *An Act Respecting the Protection of Personal Information in the Private Sector* stipulates that every person carrying on a business who holds a file on another person must, at the request of the person concerned, confirm the existence of the file and communicate to the person any personal information concerning him. British Columbia imposes a similar disclosure obligation. Its *Personal Information Protection Act* requires that upon request of an individual, an organization must provide the individual with the following: the individual's personal information under the control of the organization; information about the ways in which the personal information has been and is being used by the organization; and the names of the individuals and organizations to whom the personal information has been disclosed by the organization. Alberta's *Personal Information Protection Act* contains a nearly identical provision.

Often employers will have separate files for employees, with a file that contains any information which the employer would not want the employee to be able to access. Generally, the issue of employee access is non-contentious and employers grant access to employees through policies or as a matter of course.

27. REQUIRED NOTICES AND POSTINGS

27.1. Overview

Required notices and postings are determined by each province. Some provinces require the employer to post government issued posters and information on employee rights.

Nearly all provinces mandate occupational health and safety postings in the workplace. Often, the province will require that the employer post the entire health and safety legislation or have it readily accessible to employees who request it. Some provinces may require, depending on the number of employees, that employers post information on the names and work locations of joint health and safety committee members. These committees are a statutory requirement under both federal and provincial jurisdictions. Comprised of workers and management representatives, the committees develop and promote health and safety initiatives and make recommendations to management regarding safety protocol. Employers may be required to post information about the proper procedures in the event of an accident and bulletins informing employees about their employment-related rights at work. All such information should be displayed in areas that are clearly visible or easily accessible to each employee.

In addition, employers must comply with the WHMIS. WHMIS is a Canada-wide system designed to give employers and workers information about hazardous materials used in the workplace. Employers in workplaces with hazardous materials are required to identify those materials, ensure that proper data sheets on the materials are readily available and containers are properly labelled, and make sure that employees are properly trained on the handling and use of the materials. Employers should inform employees about hazardous materials in the workplace and make the WHMIS regulations under the provincial occupational health and safety acts readily available. Employers should review provincial employment standards, labour relations, human rights, and occupation health and safety legislation to ensure that the specific requirements for each province are satisfied.

27.2. Checklist of Do's and Don'ts

- Do verify the posting requirements for each jurisdiction.
- Do ensure that copies of the postings are prominent and available in more than one location.

www.ingramcontent.com/pod-product-compliance
Lightning Source LLC
Chambersburg PA
CBHW071355230926
51846CB00002B/563
* 9 7 8 9 0 4 1 1 5 6 3 7 2 *